Water Exercise Handbook

Lyn Hickey

First published in the United Kingdom in 2017 by

The Cloister House Press

ISBN 978-1-909456-58-9

Welcome to the Water Exercise Handbook.

The idea of this handbook is that you keep it and use it as a reference book, not only for your course but as you progress through your teaching.

Fill in the sections as you try out the exercises as you go along. You can always refer to it at a later date when you need a bit of inspiration.

Each section has a completed lesson plan and photographs of all the exercises. There are additional completed lesson plans as you get to be more adventurous and additional exercises that are not on the lesson plans!

The beginning will help keep things simple, getting more adventurous as you progress.

Practice the exercises in the water, add the progressions and see what it feels like. Then practice your demonstrations on land, preferably to the music you will be using.

Safety, yours and your participant's is paramount, but I cannot take any responsibility for any injuries incurred whist using the exercises, safe execution of each exercise and any equipment involved is your responsibility as the instructor.

Have fun, enjoy what you do, keep it effective and your participants will enjoy it to.

Lyn

Contents

Reasons to Exercise in Water

There are many reasons to exercise in water. It is good for both the body and the mind of the participants. This is due to the unique way the body reacts in the water and the actual properties of water. Water exercise is safe and effective.

Let's look at these reasons and what makes them so special.

Cooling

Unlike exercising on land, exercising in the water cools the body temperature down very quickly - the pool water temperature being in the region of 28° - 30° Celsius.

The human body temperature is usually around 37° Celsius.

The normal body temperature needs to be maintained otherwise the participants will get cold very quickly, the muscles will be cool and long lever exercises with cool muscles will cause injury.

Staying Warm

As the muscles warm up and start to exercise, the body warms up. Heat is produced by working muscles. This heat travels outwards to the skin and is released as sweat from the skin.

The pool water washes over the skin, and as the skin makes contact with the cooler water it cools down (conduction).

Although this helps the body to exercise harder and for longer, to produce heat in the body the body needs to move more and the body needs to keep moving at a level that is sufficient to stay warm in water. This requires a certain amount of effort. Therefore, it uses more calories in maintaining this effort to keep warm.

How much heat is produced is dependent on how much effort is put in (energy used).

How much effort (calories used) is dependent on the individual's fitness level, gender, body size, body shape, objective and attitude to exercise.

If the participants are working at a level of intensity suitable for their own body they will be warm and they will sweat during water exercise. Only the face will feel the effects, which can be cooled instantly by a splash of water. This is another benefit for people who do not like to feel hot and sweaty either through choice or for a medical reason i.e. the menopausal hot flushes or high blood pressure.

Reduced Impact Due to Buoyancy

Exercising in water also helps to protect the joints from jolting (impact).

Buoyancy is the name of the upward force found in water which opposes the downward pull of gravity found on land.

Working against buoyancy means the impact felt through the ankles, knees, hips and lower back when exercising on land is greatly reduced by the cushioning effect of buoyancy.

When working in water up to the waist there is approximately 50% buoyancy cushioning and when working up to the neck there is approximately 90% cushioning. The deeper the body is submerged lessens the amount of weight the person has to support. This is a major benefit of exercising in water for everybody, especially for people who have health/joint issues.

Obviously working in the deep water has no impact at all, as the feet are not able to touch the pool floor. (See the Deep Water section for more info page 176).

This reduced impact on the joints is great for protecting them from injury and protecting existing injuries or conditions providing that the body is in the correct depth of water.

An upright body in deep water

Using Archimedes' Principle. *"Anybody completely or partially submerged in fluid (water) is acted upon by an upward force which is equal to the weight of the fluid displaced by the body".*

A little bit of physics now: The weight of the submerged body parts equals the upward force of the weight of the displaced water. The deeper you are in the water, the less you weigh. The less you weigh the less impact on joints and connective tissue.

The buoyancy effect (the upward force) can been seen when dropping a non-floating object into a pool and watching it slowly and gently descend to the pool floor, much slower and gentler than if you dropped the same object on land. The denser the object the quicker it will reach the bottom of the pool, but still slower than on land.

Centre of Gravity & Centre of Buoyancy Alignment

The centre of gravity (the centre of mass) in the human body is about 55% of the body height.

This is where the weight is equally balanced, left, right, above and below this point. This is the stabilising point of the body.

When the body gets partially submerged in the water, Archimedes' Principle comes into effect.

The centre of buoyancy, usually found mid chest, needs to stay aligned directly above the centre of gravity for stability. If the two points become unaligned, the body will tilt and muscle balance will be compromised.

This is especially important for deep water and suspended exercises as the support base (standing on the pool floor) is not available.

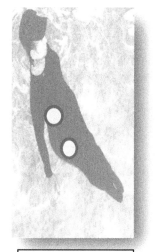

A tilted body in deep water

The first picture (page 6) is of a perfectly aligned stabilised body, centre of buoyancy directly over centre of gravity. The two blue dots are directly in line - one directly under the other.

In this picture the hips have come forward with the leg movement and the trunk has tilted backwards to balance the hips. The two blue dots are now not in a vertical line.

The centre of gravity has shifted forward slightly and the centre of buoyancy has moved backwards. The stability has been lost and the body is now out of alignment.

The actual amount of buoyancy of the human   body, is dependent on a couple of factors, mainly   body type and gender.

Body Type Differences In Water Exercise

There are three main "body" types - endomorph, mesomorph and ectomorph, although most people will have characteristics of more than one.

People who have more adipose tissue (fat) displace more water and have far greater buoyancy. These are 'apple' shapes with a tendency to be overweight. This body type is known as endomorph. This type of body will have to work harder and put in more effort (calories burned) to work against the buoyancy.

A body that is muscular with broad shoulders and a narrow waist measurement is known as mesomorph. This type will not have the same challenges with buoyancy as muscles weigh more than fat and their weight alone will help counteract some of the buoyancy.

Long and lean people with little body fat or bulging muscles and who have a high metabolic rate are known as ectomorphs. As they have very little fat, they will not have to put in as much effort as the endomorphs do to work against the buoyancy, but they do not have the muscle weight like the mesomorphs to help them.

In general females tend to be more buoyant than males because of the differences in distribution of body fat (a bigger bust and bottom).

It is important that every person exercising in water has the water level over their belly button at an absolute minimum. Exercising in water below this depth does not give enough buoyancy so the impact is much greater, like running without shoes on.

Working Opposite Muscles Due To Buoyancy

On land we live with gravity (a downward pull). In the water we have buoyancy (an upward force) that works in opposition to gravity. Therefore, every downward movement is a buoyancy resisted movement.

The downward movement is harder in the water than on land because of the buoyancy's upward force and reduced gravity's downward pull. Therefore, more force (energy) is required for each downward movement.

The opposite muscle will be doing the majority of the work. For example, a high kick on land is led by the quadriceps muscles pulling the leg upwards against the downward pull of gravity. The force of gravity helps return the leg back to a standing position helping the hamstring muscles.

In water the buoyancy (upward force) helps the leg upwards and the hamstring muscles have to work harder to return the leg to a standing position, pulling down through the upward force of buoyancy. This is known as buoyancy resisted movements.

With a change of body position and different exercise the quadriceps can be worked just as hard as the hamstrings. This gives all of the muscle groups a total body workout. (see exercise breakdown).

Muscle Toning
Working out in the water is one of the safest ways to tone up the muscles, because they work against the resistance of the water. As water is so much thicker than air, it is harder to move through. In the water muscle pairs can be worked at the same time. The muscles have to contract and put in more effort to push and pull the water. The legs have to work harder to move through the thickness of the water.

The more area presented (wide hand rather than a balled up fist) takes up more space, so has to move more water, which in turn takes more effort for the muscles.

Arm exercises can be made easier by slicing the water with a flat hand in a horizontal position or a vertical position in an upwards and downwards movement, depending on the exercise. Alternatively, they can be made harder by increasing frontal resistance by using a flat hand in the vertical position for push pull exercises and a horizontal position for upward and downward movements.

The same principle applies to leg exercises. Using a long leg kick is much harder than a bent leg kick. The longer the limb, the more water that has to move, the harder work.

This can be made harder still by creating turbulence. When moving forward the water that has just moved out of the way goes around the body and meets more water coming in the direction the body has just moved from (eddy currents).

If the body turns or tries to move backwards it has to deal with the water moving against it, so even greater effort is required to carry on moving. The water will try to stop the movement for a couple of seconds and as the body keep exercising it will have to increase the intensity to move through it.

Exercises can be made more intense by using 'aqua equipment'.

More about using "aqua equipment" on Page 233.

Core Control
Even if you stood in a pool without anyone else there, you would need a certain amount of core control to remain standing upright. The pool's circulation pump filling the pool and the skimmers taking the water back into the system cause some movement. If you are not in the correct body position you can waiver slightly. Now consider the rest of the aqua class participants. There are more people moving about in the water and water moving about at different speeds and in different directions. Each person creates turbulence.

Body Alignment
Correct body posture is absolutely essential. The abdominal muscles need to be engaged at all times. Shoulders and hips need to stay in a vertical line. This protects the muscles of your back and allows you to exercise correctly and safely. This has the added benefit of strengthening the stomach muscles for the entire session. Arms and legs are moved in opposition in water exercise to help keep the body in this alignment. Various arm movements will help stabilise the body.

Fat Burning
In the heart and lungs section previously, we explained how the heart does not have to beat as fast as in a land class, keeping the heart rate down a little. You exercise but stay in your aerobic

training zone, which can be anything from 55% (unfit) to 80% (fit) of your maximum heart rate.

Why the maths? If you have a goal, i.e. to lose weight, change shape or just get fitter, your body needs progressive overload. As the body gets used to a certain level of workout, it then needs to up the effort a little bit to move onto the next level. The easiest way to monitor this is by heart rate - the true indicator of how hard you are working. The way to do this is not complicated.

Use the figure 220 minus your age. Multiply by 55% and minus 7 for working out in water. This figure is the lower end of your aerobic training zone. You need to work out hard enough for your heart to beat that many times a minute. Any lower and the exercise is not as beneficial. Repeat the maths, this time 220 minus your age multiply by 80%, minus 15 for exercising in water. This figure is the top end of your aerobic training zone. Your heart rate should NOT go above this figure to stay working aerobically.

Because we are working against the resistance of the water which is harder to move through than air, we will always be working aerobically and for this our bodies must use the fat to make energy as its main fuel source. That's what makes exercising in water a fat burning exercise.

To check that everyone is working in the right zone, we can use various ways. Teach the participants RPE, keep it simple, on a scale of 1 – 10 how hard are you working, 10 being the max they can do. Ask them if they can work a little harder, keep giving the progressions to exercises and see how many take them.

Or the talk test, if they can say a short sentence then they are probably in the right zone, if they can tell you their life story then they probably need to work harder. If they can hardly speak to you, then they are definitely working at a too higher rate.

Heart and Lungs

Your heart works harder as you exercise because your muscles need more oxygen to keep them working. In general, your heart rate increases, you breathe harder to increase the amount of air and oxygen you need. The amount and the speed of the blood pumped around your body increases to deliver this oxygen and remove the carbon dioxide that the body naturally makes. Like muscles working harder to tone up, your heart and lungs are getting a work out too.

Exactly the same happens when you exercise in water, but the hydrostatic pressure (the body stocking) helps squeeze the blood back to the heart through the veins and valves in the legs, so the heart does not have to work quite as hard. The heart rate still increases but not to the same extent that it would in a land class. Because of this extra help from the hydrostatic pressure, the heart rate will be in the region of 7 to 15 beats lower per minute. This is excellent news for any one with high blood pressure.

The intercostal muscles in the chest cavity will have to work harder when covered by the water because of the hydrostatic pressure, this is due to the direct pressure on the chest. To inflate the lungs, the chest has to expand through this additional pressure, so they get an additional work out that is not possible on land. People suffering from asthma should be careful in deep water only classes, as they have no means of relieving this pressure. In shallow water classes they can work with the chest submerged and then stand upright to relieve the pressure if necessary.

Pressure Diuresis
Due to the cooler temperature of the water and the three dimensional pressure of the hydrostatic pressure, blood volume increases the kidney pressure which increases the volume of urine. Combined with exercise the body can dehydrate if fluids are not taken during and after exercise. This is one of the reasons that pool users always need a visit to the loo immediately after getting out of the water. Rehydrating immediately after a session is recommended.

Lymphatic Drainage
Hydrostatic pressure helps the lymphatic system move the lymph fluid. As this system has no pump of its own, it works by muscle movement and blood flow. Lymph fluid can only flow in one direction.

We know the hydrostatic pressure helps blood flow back to the heart. This, in turn, helps the lymphatic fluid return any excess fluid to the blood stream and toxins to the lymph nodes situated around the body. As the lymphatic system makes the cells which protect our immunity and remove toxins from our body, it is important that this system is kept in good working order.

Joint Support and Hydrostatic Pressure

All joints that are under the water are protected by the hydrostatic pressure. This is a 3 dimensional pressure which acts like a support body stocking. The joints are encased in this pressure which supports them through their normal range of movement. If a joint has an injury, the hydrostatic pressure will support the joint capsule and hold it in place (like a support bandage) allowing it to move freely within its range without the risk of further damage and keeping the joint mobile.

Participant's Safety and Screening

This of course is the most important factor in water exercise.

Health checks (participant screening) need to be completed at the start of every class. Some participants will have completed a written PARQ (physical activity readiness questionnaire) but unless you have access to this information which is highly confidential and should be kept under lock and key; you have no alternative but to speak to your participants.

It is ideal to check their health on a 1-2-1 basis before they get in the water, especially for any new participants. For regulars that you have been teaching for a while a blanket question will cover you, such as "Has everyone told me anything I need to know or any changes to health since last time?". It's for *their* safety and you need to teach them to inform you, even if it's just their medication has changed or they have had a bad cold or infection.

You need to know about these issues and do not be afraid to ask: You cannot give them safe exercises if you do not know about their state of health.

If the participant has a medical issue you are not qualified to teach you must refer them to an instructor who is, i.e. an instructor with a G.P Referral or Cardiac qualification.

When to say No

If you are in any doubt, or are unsure about any of the participant's medical issues, you must refer them back to their health carer.

It is your duty to do so, and keep them safe.

There are few issues that require referral but if in doubt do not take the risk.

This is not a complete list but some of the more common ailments and issues.

- **Complicated pregnancy**
- **Identical Twins**
- **Multiple pregnancy**
- **Chest pains**
- **Recent stomach bugs**
- **Uncontrolled diabetes**
- **Severe COPD**
- **Early stages of cardiac rehabilitation**
- **Open wounds**
- **Unstable sugar levels**
- **Feeling unwell on the day**
- **Rashes**
- **Shingles**
- **Any issues you are unsure of**

Support

During the 1-2-1 screening process, it is also a good time to find out your participant's name, exactly how confident they are in the water, or if they are not confident at all, so they can be placed properly.

Any information you can get which will help you break down any barriers they may have to exercise and make them feel part of the group. In order for them to give you commitment and return regularly, you must give them commitment and individual support.

What are their reasons for exercising? Do they have any specific goals? Have they come on their own? Do they have any concerns about exercising? Are they water confident? What are their fitness levels like?

Injury

Exercising in water is great for joint and muscle injuries. The hydrostatic pressure (the body stocking again) acts as a support bandage and allows the joint to work through its natural range whilst being supported, helping the muscles to strengthen. If the injured joint or muscle is in the lower part of the body, the reduced impact of the buoyancy will help to alleviate any jarring. Any swelling around the joint will be compressed by the hydrostatic pressure, reducing the swelling while in the water

Oedema

The hydrostatic pressure will also reduce any swelling (oedema) of the joint by compression (again the support bandage). This will encourage the excess fluid to move through the lymphatic system by muscle movement. It is irrelevant whether the swelling is due to injury, poor circulation, inflammation or pregnancy.

Hypertension

The hydrostatic pressure will also help to reduce blood pressure. The three dimensional pressure helps the blood return to the heart with added ease.

It acts by squeezing against the body so the blood in the veins is pushed upwards through the valves and towards the heart. The heart and circulatory system do not have to work against gravity while in the water, so the heart does not have to work so hard in maintaining blood flow.

On initial entry into the water, the hydrostatic pressure may push the blood upwards more quickly than if it were flowing upwards on land and increase the blood pressure by spiking it. It is important for people suffering with high blood pressure or who are on beta blockers (medication to lower the heart rate) to start moving immediately they enter the water to allow the body to adjust as quickly as possible. Just stepping up and down in the water will suffice.

Reduces Depression and Stress

The hypothalamus gland in the brain is the control centre of the body's emotions, feelings, stress and hormone production and control, amongst other things. It is closely linked with the pituitary gland, also in the brain. The nervous tissue of the hypothalamus is the communication link between the endocrine system and the nervous system. The nervous system produces impulses that travel through the nerves and the endocrine system produces chemicals or hormones directly into the blood.

The brain and spinal cord has many opioid receptors. When exercising hard a chain reaction starts.

The hypothalamus asks the pituitary gland for endorphins, the pituitary gland then releases its own chemical which travels around the body until the chemicals reach the neurons which contain the endorphins.

The endorphins are then released into the blood and travel to the opioid receptors in the brain. This causes the feel good factor that hard exercise brings, but you need to work out to receive this reward. Each person is individual with different amount of opioid receptors and a different idea and capacity of exercising hard.

The feel good factor (endorphin release) makes you feel better and when this becomes a regular occurrence, your emotions stabilise.

Joint Problems
People with finger, wrist, elbow injuries or arthritis are not advised to use any hand held equipment as the constant grip can cause them joint pain. Keep hands in a comfortable position and change this position as much as possible. Some participants like to use the neoprene webbed mitts if they have finger problems. The stitching can be removed between the fingers appropriate to the participant's needs.

Lower back issues
Keep correct body position and leg kick low. If they are water confident try to keep them in chest height water to reduce the impact even further. Make sure their abdominal muscles are fully engaged throughout.

Hip Replacements
The participant needs clearance from their health provider / consultant before coming back to exercise.

Go back to basics with the lower body and do not allow the participant to attempt any wide leg movements, sidekicks, wide jacks, any crossing over the mid line exercises etc. that may destabilise the new hip.

Work with forward and backward exercises at low intensity. The aim is to rebuild the strength in the quadriceps and glutes muscles, along with gentle exercises for the abductors and adductors as soon as the participant has medical clearance. Usually another 6 weeks after being cleared to exercise.

Knee Replacements
Again the participant needs clearance from their health provider / consultant before coming back to exercise.

Small movements forward and backwards, keeping the knee joint soft at all times and any "hamstring curl" type exercise can only be done within the participant's limitation. The main aim is to build up the quadriceps and hamstring muscles again.

Diabetics

Keep a special eye on them. Make sure they have their reviver drink on pool side within easy reach.

If they are not following the exercises and seem a little confused, they may be in need of a sugar fix. Most diabetics know how exercise affects their blood sugar levels and take steps to avoid a dip during/after class, but this does not always go to plan.

Note: diabetics should always wear socks or pool shoes while exercising in the water as the nerve endings in the feet can become desensitised and they don't always feel any scrapes or cuts they may get from the bottom of the pool.

Disabled

Having a disability does not prevent exercise, but in the water a disabled participant's body balance may be affected. In addition, it may be more challenging to find the point of centre of balance.

The body will tend to roll towards the side of the disabled limb, disturbing the alignment of the centre of gravity and the centre of buoyancy.

With practice the individual will find their own balance by making some adjustments to the exercises with your help.

Asthmatics

All asthmatics must have their inhaler on poolside, somewhere where you or someone else knows where it is, as they may not be able to explain where it is if they are having an asthma attack.

The hydrostatic pressure causes the chest muscles to work harder than on land, so deep water exercises are not advised. Asthmatics need to be able to move to shallower water where the chest is not covered if they feel their breathing is getting difficult.

Asthmatics must be prepared and so must you the instructor. It does not matter how well controlled the asthma is, there is always a possibility of an attack. Keep an eye on your asthmatic participants always. Know where their inhaler is and notify the lifeguard.

COPD

(Chronic Obstructive Pulmonary Disease).
Deep water exercise is not advised; anyone with COPD should have medical clearance to exercise and have the water level under their chest.

The hydrostatic pressure can become a problem if the person's chest is constantly submerged; COPD sufferers find breathing difficult and the hydrostatic pressure will make it harder for them to breathe. This could cause major problems.

Pregnancy

This is a complicated area. Whilst the water is one of the best places for mum to be to exercise in, there are a great many considerations to be observed.

The participant should obtain medical clearance before starting or continuing to exercise.

From conception, a hormone called "relaxin" becomes present. This hormone does exactly what its name states, and it relaxes the connective tissues in the body; the entire body.

If the participant is not used to regular **water exercises** they **do not** start doing so in the 1st three months of their pregnancy!

As soon as you know they are pregnant you need to make adaptions for the presence of the relaxin hormone. Any excessive resistance can cause shoulder, elbow, wrist, knee, hip and ankle issues.

Hand held equipment is not advised, due to the larger surface area of the equipment creating extra resistance which needs more force from the shoulders and the elbows. The constant grip can stress the joints in the wrist and hands.

The pelvic area can become unstable as the baby grows, so wide leg exercises are to be avoided.
Due to the viscosity (thickness) of the water, turning and twisting are also to be avoided, especially as the baby grows.

Rebound movements can become uncomfortable for the mum to be as the breasts enlarge and the bump gets bigger. The breasts should always be kept under the water's surface.

Obviously abdominal exercises are also to be avoided, as now is not the time to tighten the abdominal muscles.

Make sure mum to be keeps a constant watch on you, and you on her, so she will know what exercises are contraindicated and you can give her alternatives.

A pre and post-natal water exercise specific course is essential if you want to teach this as a specialist class.

Post Natal
Clearance from the midwife or doctor is essential; clearance timing will be determined by the birth and any complications.

As a general rule start easy and build up strength gradually.

Older population
They maybe on a cocktail of medication, and have a few health issues. They need to work at a level that suits them; they also need to feel that they are achieving some benefits.

They are often worried that they hold the rest of the class up as they perceive themselves to be slower and not able to do it all. They are capable of doing what they can do and need as much encouragement as everybody else.

Body positioning is very important and not too many reps of one exercise. Try to keep all working joints submerged if they are water confident.

Frail People
Avoid water turbulence as they may not have the core strength to cope and it may knock them off their feet.
Also avoid added resistance equipment other than a noodle which they can use to help keep their balance if needed.

Keep them in the shallow water just above belly button height and ensure they work at a level that is comfortable for them individually.

14 – 16 year olds
At this age their bodies are still growing,

The use of noodles equipment is permitted as they are the lightest resistance, preferably used for fun and balance, and to promote exercise encouragement, but no other resistance equipment should be used.

Their own body weight, strength and force are enough to achieve training results in a safe and controlled way.

For this age group to be engaged there needs to be a certain element of fun involved.

Many pools will only allow clients less than 16 years of age to participate in aqua session if accompanied by an adult, and it is usually mum. It's a great benefit for them as it is non-competitive and the body insecurities are minimal due to the lack of boys their age attending and the fact they are covered by the water.

You will need to check with your or the pools insurance company to teach under 16s just to ensure you are fully covered.

All Fitness Levels

Everyone who exercises in water works at their own fitness level. There is no competition to keep up with or do as much as the person next to them. The instructor offers progressions (harder exercises) for anyone who wants to do them. It's very difficult for the participant to see what the person next to them is doing, because the water is moving about. The participants do the exercise at a speed that suits them, and they do as many repetitions as they want to or can do.

You the instructor will motivate and keep an eye on correct body position. Some days the participants may feel like working hard, other days maybe not so hard. Water exercise is all about them and how they feel at any particular session.

Because of the hydrostatic pressure in the water, blood pooling does not happen. When you get tired on land exercise and you stop, there is the possibility of the blood pooling in the lower legs which can make you dizzy. In water the participants can stop, but to remain warm they are encouraged to just keep moving the legs slowly.

Many marathon runners, tri athletes and sports professionals train in water because of the resistance which makes the exercises harder and consequently builds up the strength and endurance in the muscles. But for most of us, we want to exercise at our own level, be motivated to push ourselves a little harder and reach our own personal goals, whatever they may be.

All Ages

You will get a very mixed age group within the aqua session - some mums in their 40s bring their daughters in their teens; some mid 20s – 30s who bring their partners; 50+, 60+ and 70+. Age is no barrier to exercising in water. The age group depends very much on what time of day the sessions are. Obviously people who are working during the day cannot attend day sessions, so may attend the evening ones.

Regardless of their age, everyone who attends a class needs to get a good work out to their own ability, in line with their personal goals and current fitness level.

Non and Weak Swimmers

Water exercise is suitable for non-swimmers and weak swimmers, but a shallow water class is essential. They must stay in a depth where their feet can touch the floor easily.

You as the instructor will need to give an alternative exercise when you are demonstrating a both feet off the floor (suspended) exercise. As a participant you should take this alternative if you are not confident with both of your feet off the floor at the same time.

To exercise fully you need to be relaxed in the water. For nervous participants, it is best to be positioned close to the side of the pool at all times, let the instructor know if you are not confident in the water, so they can keep a special eye on you. A noodle may help with your stability until you get more core control or are more confident in the water.

Social

Water exercise has always been a social event, with some classes being exactly that, a meeting place for a 'little exercise' and a lot of chat. Times have changed. Over the past 10 years the 'chat' has become an after class social over a cup of tea, and beneficial exercise has taken priority in many sessions.

Due to the resistance (the thickness) of the water everyone is working at their own personal pace, unlike many land based exercise classes where everyone follows the instructor at a set speed.

Working at a set speed (unless it is very slow) is not possible in the water due to our differing body types, muscle weight, strength, fitness level and the amount of fat (adipose tissue) we each have.

All these make it harder to move through the thickness of the water.

So exercises are completed in repetitions, sometimes a few exercises will be linked together, but still done in repetitions, and it is up to the individual how many they actually do.

This can allow the focus of exercise to be side-lined and a quick comment turns into a full blown conversation while still doing exercise but at a minimal level.

A lot will depend on the age group of the class and their individual focus. Many classes will work hard in the water, and then get together for a social afterwards. Their friendships bond and lead to lunches / outings together (often with the instructor included). The nonattendance of one participant is often explained by another. The social aspect far outreaches the exercise class itself.

For some people, the class is the only exercise they can do and the people there are the only people they ever see, so conversation is important. Like ante/post-natal classes, they have a lot to chat about.

Each class takes on a special atmosphere of its own. Some classes completely focus and they are there to exercise while for others chatting is more important. As an instructor you will get to know this and develop your own style of classes.

Fun
Exercising in the water can be fun. Working out to music can be motivating. You are working at a level that suits you and you have no pressure to keep up with anyone else but are surrounded by likeminded people. It's a little bit of 'me' time away from the realities of every day stresses. It's a time to switch off. Focus on the feel of the water, the music and the instructor.

Discreet
Some people do not like having their body on show, others do not like the feeling they could be watched whilst exercising; some are just body conscious for personal reasons. Very few people are really happy with their own body. It's the world we live in today where pictures are photo shopped to make the perfect image. We all have areas that we want to improve, areas we wish were better.

With exercising in water your body is covered. For some participants their lack of co-ordination is a bother, but under the water it doesn't matter; we don't have complicated choreography and tiny dance moves to remember and the only person who can see what is happening is the instructor.

The Pool Depth

This is a tricky one as the ideal pool depth depends on the person in it. Some people are tall, others are quite short. Either way the water should be above their navel (at an absolute minimum) otherwise they will have sore legs and lower back issues due to the impact of the weight of the body and the pool floor.

There is not enough buoyancy to make water exercises safe if the water level is below the navel.

The ideal for most people is having the water level around chest height. This is, of course, providing they are confident in the water. This depth allows all working muscles to be submerged and supported throughout the exercise. This is **shallow water**. If the participant cannot touch the floor, then the exercises are **deep water**.

Pool Water Temperature

Water temperature varies from pool to pool; the big 4 or 6 lane 25 or 50 metre pools were designed for swimming in. The water temperature in them will be about 28°/ 29°C; teaching pools often too shallow for water exercise will be about 30°C and lagoon pools often a little higher.

Your session plan will need changing for the different water temperatures and the different pools that you teach in. The colder the water, the longer it will take for the body to warm up, and low level exercises will just allow the body to chill quickly. In warmer water, high level exercises may cause dehydration and other heat related illnesses very quickly.

Occasionally things go wrong with pools, so you need to be able to adapt your plans at a moment's notice.

You may arrive at your usual pool to find the boiler has broken down or a backwash has just been done and they are still refilling the pool. The water that was 30°C has now gone down to 28°C. In this case, you will need a longer warm up, more aerobic exercises and to keep everyone moving so they don't get cold.

Or very occasionally the water has been heated up for a baby session or the pool equipment has gone into overdrive and what is normally 29°C is now 31°C. Great for a relaxing, stretching and Pilates/yoga type session with slow long lever controlled movements, but beware of your participants overheating.

So always have a backup plan! And encourage participants to bring plastic bottled water onto poolside and actually drink it throughout the session.

Pool Water Clarity, the pool water is not your responsibility but you need to be aware of clarity, the general rule is if you cannot see the bottom of the pool, you cannot teach in it. Take advice from pool management. Also smell and colour, anything different even slightly, check with the management to ensure it is safe to use.

You the instructor

You need to make eye contact and watch every participant all the time, for many reasons.

All participants should be fairly confident in the water depth they are in, even if they cannot swim. Look out for the ones who panic when they get their face splashed, or those who are afraid of going under the water, just in case they slip.

To see if they are working at the right level for them, if they are becoming very flushed (red in the face) they may be over doing it too quickly and need to step it down a bit.

Look out for anyone who seems to be in pain, especially in the chest, right arm or shoulder. If this happens remove them from the water immediately and get urgent medical back up through your emergency action plan straight away. It is much easier to deal with a heart problem outside of the pool rather than in it.

Your participants need space to exercise at each side and in front and behind. Too close together and they will inadvertently kick or hit each other. Keep an eye on the ones that travel while exercising so they don't bump into anyone.

Beware of the anti-splash ropes which will spin if held onto to and can pinch quite badly. It is best to keep your participants away from them.

If the pool is shared with swimmers, keep the class forward from the dividing line. Some swimmers splash; some have a wide leg kick which will be a very unwelcome surprise if the people in the back of the class get kicked as the swimmer passes.

Look out for body position. Exercising in the wrong body position can cause injury. Keep correcting all through the class. Nag them; it is for their own good! Occasionally you will encounter a person who totally ignores you, but most participants will learn to check their own position every time you mention it.

Keep all working muscle groups and joints under the water. This will give the joint support and resistance to work against.

As we have said, water exercise is good for nearly everyone providing you as the instructor abide by the safety rules. Don't try to introduce exercises that are meant for land classes. Most land exercises are ineffective in the water as they work against gravity.

Holding on to the pool side and exercising is dangerous! It puts the shoulder out of alignment, makes the fingers and wrist tense, increases blood pressure and besides, there are safer ways to do the same exercises and with better results.

Hauling the body up on pool side as in push ups or triceps dips are also dangerous! The pool side is a wet slippery surface and it is all too easy for someone to misjudge the distance or not have the strength in their upper body and consequently slip and smash their jaw/face/coccyx into the concrete. Your insurance company will not be happy.

Arms out of the water, obviously we need to stretch upwards, but this is a 20 second movement. We don't have the issue of blood pooling, but we do have an issue with exercises that raise the arms out of the water. This falsely elevates the heart rate; there is no water resistance for raised arms, unless they are sitting on the pool floor, which we definitely do NOT recommend. All arm exercises need to be under the water to be effective. Many of your participants will have high blood pressure, so raised arms are not safe for them and totally ineffective for everyone else.

For maximum safety every person in the water works at their own speed and puts in as much effort as they feel able to. Encouragement is great but within boundaries.

Explain to your class that you want to get the best from them, but within their own capabilities. Do not let them compete with each other. It's their workout just for them, they may be in a group but it's their individual goals that are being met. They are to work at their own speed and their own effort.

Instructor Safety

Keep your fluids with you, and actually drink them. Pool side temperature can get to 33°C + with very high humidity, dehydration is a concern for both you and your participants..

Also wear suitable clothing that your limbs can been seen in, ideally of breathable material and a pair of decent old clean trainers that will cushion your joints from impact from a concrete floor. Keep these trainers for pool side use only. The pool chemical chlorine will destroy the glue in your trainers and make them smell, so they won't last very long. It is dangerous for you to demonstrate barefoot. Even on a mat, the impact is so great you will get injured.

The pool area, including mats if you use them, could be very slippery. Do not take any risks! It is important that your posture is correct and your core engaged to help you prevent a fall.

It is unsafe for you to demonstrate in the water if you cannot see each and every one of your participants' legs and faces at the same time.

If you do not have an overall view of everyone, you cannot tell what they are doing, or the level they are working at. They also cannot see your legs, so your demonstrations are useless.

In addition, if you are in the water teaching and something happens to a participant, you may not notice until the people either side of them notify you. Valuable time will have been wasted especially if it's a heart attack or a stroke.

For the safety of your class! Please stay on the poolside. Even if you have a lifeguard with you, they can affect a rescue and will probably see a problem before you do.

No matter how many pools you teach in, make sure you know the pool's EAP (Emergency Action Plan). Each pool will have one and they will be significantly different.

If you have a lifeguard they will deal with any alarms, or raise an alarm if necessary. You need to deal with your class as stated in the centres EAP. So it is imperative that you know the emergency exits and the protocol for fire alarms and pool alarms. The lifeguard will direct you as to which exit to use, when to use it and issue space blankets (foil sheets).

If you do not have a lifeguard you will need to know the emergency procedures of a "water incident"; where the pool alarms are; who will respond to the alarm and when. You also need to know the fire exits and the different sound of the fire alarm; which person is responsible for evacuation and who gives out the space blankets should a full evacuation be necessary.

Either way, on hearing any alarm, you should stop your class and be ready to clear the pool. The lifeguard or whoever is in charge will instruct you what to do with your class.

The RLSS (Royal Life Saving Society) run a course for teachers (swimming) and aqua instructors in rescue and you only need to learn how to affect a rescue at the maximum pool depth you teach in.

Although this is not a legal requirement, it's a useful certification to have along with your first aid. Your first aid certificate is a legal requirement for most pools.

Pool Side Demonstrations
The exercises are designed for use in water. This can make them very high impact for the instructor who is demonstrating them on a concrete pool side. The pool area can be very hot and humid, unlike an air conditioned studio. Dress *appropriately*. A swimsuit, or swim shorts (for men) are inappropriate. The eye line of your class is usually the lower half of your body's trunk!

- It's not your workout!
- You are there to demonstrate, motivate and correct.
- Use your personality to make sure the class is fun.
- Use your knowledge to make sure the class is effective.

- Use your fitness experience to make sure that their body positions are correct at all times.
- Do not be afraid to correct body positions.

Once you have demonstrated 6 to 8 times and everyone is doing it, use the rest of the time to motivate, encourage bigger exercises at a greater speed; ask the participants if they are working; give progressions; monitor their level; look out for problems; give teaching points and correct any errors that you see before the countdown (seconds) to the next move. By constantly reminding your participants of correct body positioning, eventually it will come naturally most of the time.

Your demonstrations need to be big, exaggerated and powerful so everyone can see them and not just the two font rows. It's advisable to change your teaching position, again and again to give all participants the opportunity to observe you from all angles.

Use your voice - change its tone, motivate,issue teaching points and encouragement. Correct body positions and smile.

You cannot work to the speed of your music; you need to demonstrate at a speed that is of the fastest person in the water. The music is to motivate and enjoy. If you use 125-128 bpm speed you may find it's not motivating enough for all your classes. If you use 132-135 it may be too fast.

You as the instructor set the speed and power of each exercise, as long as their body position is correct and they are using full lever exercise, the participants will set their own speed.

Choose your music *carefully* and change it regularly, like your exercises. No one wants to do the same thing over and over again for weeks. Once the class know what exercise goes with what track they will have switched off and lost focus and there will be no progression.

Chit chatting in the session is distracting for others around the chit chatters; also the chit chatters are not focused on what they are doing. In some sessions the participants like to sing along. As they are working aerobically, singing during certain sections is perfectly acceptable.

At least you know they are breathing fully if they are singing, especially for the toning exercises, but not so much for the short lever power spurts.

It's all down to you, the instructor. The class effectiveness, fun and enjoyment, not to mention their safety is all your responsibility!

Instructors 12 point check list
1) Is the area safe?
2) Do you have a lifeguard?
3) If not: do you understand the EAP for that particular pool?
4) Where are the pool alarm buttons situated? / Where are the fire exits? / Where are the emergency blankets?
5) Have you screened all your participants PARQ?
6) What is the water temperature?
7) Are you dressed appropriately, including trainers?
8) Do you have drinking water
9) Are you insured?
10) Is your music legal?
11) Do you have a plan with progressions and adaptations?
12) Are your demos big, powerful and at the proper speed?

Summing it all up
The science behind why water exercise is so effective is actually very simple.

- Buoyancy

This is just an unbalanced upwards force on the bottom of a submerged object (in the case of water exercise the feet if in a standing position, the back if in a laying position or any part of the body that is submerged and facing the pool floor). Buoyancy works in opposition to gravity. This helps reduce any impact during exercise, so the ankles, knees, hips and lower back do not get jarred.

Good for everyone but essential for anyone who is obese, injured, frail, has osteoporosis, osteoarthritis, pregnant or has a lower joint (feet, ankle knee) hip or back injury.

With buoyancy it does mean that the opposite muscles are working as opposed to the land exercise, as the power down part of the exercise is the one that is buoyancy resisted (harder). The upward movement is the one that is buoyancy assisted (easier).

- Hydrostatic Pressure

This is unique to the water, a 3 dimensional pressure which acts like a body stocking for any part of the body under the surface of the water. Its properties are as follows: aiding venous return; lowers the working heart rate; keeps the body using its aerobic energy system as the main fuel source; stimulates the kidneys; increases intercostal muscle strength; aids the lymphatic system to remove toxin from the body; supports all joint capsules that are submerged; reduces swelling; removes excess fluid at cellular level and reduces blood pressure.

- Resistance

This is due to the thickness of the water; its proper name is viscosity. Moving through the water is harder than moving through air so muscles strengthen and tone more quickly. You need more effort and burn more calories and you are working aerobically so stay in a fat burning zone. You can alter the exercise to make it harder if you want to by using a greater surface area or creating turbulence and making eddy currents/ wave drag. You can make the exercises easier by reducing the surface area, for example moving forwards is harder than moving sideways, different hand positions will also alter the surface area, as will using aqua equipment as long as it's used properly.

- Temperature

The water being cooler than the body temperature just means that the participant needs to work harder to maintain heat. The more heat generated the more calories are burnt. Long lever movements are needed to ensure the muscles work harder. Remember cooler water is washing over the skin all the time.

Planning the Exercises

So how do we actually make the exercises effective for everyone? Every movement you plan to do has to work and be effective for everyone in the session.

Before putting a bunch of exercises together you need to think of the participant's fitness levels and abilities and think of each individual movement.

Is it buoyancy resisted or a buoyancy assisted movement?

Is the movement working against the resistance of the water?

How many muscle groups are involved in the movement and what are they? The answer should be yes to the first two questions and for the last one, the muscle groups should be exercised equally to make a total body workout. If one side of a muscle group is exercised more than the other, the group can become unbalanced.

So here we go.   This is a time to remember buoyancy. The muscle group that is leading the downward movement is the one working against buoyancy, (buoyancy resisted) the muscle group in the upward movement is the one that buoyancy is helping (buoyancy assisted). So some thought is needed on how best to work both pair of muscles.

❖ Example 1: A forward leg kick:

On land this is a quads exercise as we work against gravity. But in water, it changes.

 As the leg starts to raise this is buoyancy *assisted*, helping the quads. As the leg comes back down to starting position, this is buoyancy *resisted* so the hamstrings are doing the work.

So to work the quad muscles, they need to have an exercise in pulling the leg downwards from a raised movement behind the body.

 A long lever backwards kick is one way. As the leg is pulled down through the water to the standing position, the quads are working in a buoyancy resisted movement. The hamstrings on the upward part of the backward kick are also buoyancy assisted.

❖ Example 2: A Bicep curl:

On land this is a bicep exercise again because of the gravity. But in water, this too changes.

As the hands start to come towards the shoulders, this is buoyancy assisted and the biceps are helped, as the hands lower, this is buoyancy resisted, so the triceps are doing the work.

It's only from the pool floor to water surface and from water surface back to the pool floor which is affected by buoyancy.

Resistance Moves

Any muscle group working in a backwards – forwards – sideways movement through the water is working against resistance

- ❖ Example: Pushing arms out in front and pulling hands back to chest. Provided the fingers are turned upwards, this moves the water forwards and backwards, creating turbulence and working through the resistance.

- ❖ Example: Skis, the movement forward and backwards of the legs (and arms) pushes the water in different directions creating turbulence and working through resistance.

- ❖ Example: Travelling either in a forwards, backwards or sideways motion is moving the water and is working against resistance.

Timing

Again unlike land, the reps (repetitions) have to be in a minimum of 8 - 16, this will allow all participants to complete some of them.

Many instructors work on time (20, 30, 40 seconds) rather than actual reps as various body types, fitness levels, age, sex and abilities will alter the actual number of reps that can be completed in a given amount of time.

No one can work at the same speed and the same level in water exercise because of the resistance. If the change of exercise is too quick, not everybody will have managed to do the stated number and they then get frustrated that they cannot keep up and are not getting a proper work out. Too long and it's boring.

Intensity

90% of all water exercises can be used anywhere in the session. It depends on the intensity of the exercise and length of the lever as to where they fit best and the fitness level of the participant. All warm up exercises should have at least one foot on the floor, shoulders may be under the surface for a greater intensity for the fitter participant, and the speed can be increased. For cardio work there should be rebound (bouncing movements) and shoulders under movements if the exercise is powerful (more surface area presented). For toning exercises, it depends on the fitness level of the participants, either shoulders under or if very water confident, suspended. (The feet are not touching the pool floor during that exercise). All suspended movements take a lot more effort and will also increase the heart rate to quite a high level.

Jogging
- Short lever, medium speed can be used in the warm up.
- High knees, bouncing, power arms can be used for cardio.
- High wide knees, long lever arms shoulders under the surface can be used for toning exercises.

Grouping exercises together can work if you choose carefully and allow them to be done at the participant's speed, rather than count them down. If you count down, the participants will work at your speed rather than theirs.

Grouping
Example 1.   Forward right long leg kick, backward right long leg kick, jump ¼ turn i.e. 4 reps then change working leg.

Example 2.   2 x jacks, right leg side raiser left leg side raiser and repeat for 30 seconds.

Warm Up
The warm up section must do exactly what it says - warm up the body, warm up the muscles, slightly increase core temperature, increase the fluidity of the synovial fluid in the joints, slightly increase the heart rate, increase the oxygen levels to the muscle groups, allow the mind to focus on what the body is doing rather than what is going to happen later in the day or tomorrow.

It also gives you a time where you can practise a more complicated exercise at a lower speed. In water the warm up is anything from 8 to 15 minutes, depending on the fitness level of the participants.

As the water is colder than the human body temperature, it will start to cool the body very quickly, keep as many major muscle groups working at the same time. The warm up must be comprehensive. Start with short lever exercises and gradually progress the speed and lever length as the warm up section progresses. By the end of the warm up, the heart rate should be higher than at the start, the muscles should be warm and the body ready to work out.

Unlike land exercise, all body parts need to keep moving at all times (unless the water temperature is extremely warm e.g. 32°C+). All muscle groups need to be involved and progressed gently to maintain warmth.

Upper and lower body working at the same time, usually in opposition to keep the core balanced. Progressions need to be offered with every exercise for the fitter participants.

All participants need to be watched, motivated and corrected, especially on body positions like leaning forward into the water. Abs engaged throughout. Shoulders back and down and bottoms tucked under.

Remember it's all about your participants, The PARQ (health questionnaire) verbal or form filling, refer or adaptations for those that need them, progressions for all, encouragement and corrections for all, support each person individually, because they are an individual. Interaction with you and each other is important, ask for feedback and give them feedback. I have said it before, if you know why they are there and what their goals are then it's easier for you to feedback and interact.

On the next page there is a warm up lesson plan. For more information, detailed photographs, explanations, progressions and teaching point on each exercise, go to the page number listed against that exercise. Each exercise has its own page.

As we said earlier, each exercise can be used in most of the categories of a session, and all categories for each exercise are listed under the same page.

A single ♥ signifies an easy exercise, possibly warm up
♥ ♥ how to make it harder,
♥ ♥ ♥ is usually cardio or a harder exercise
♥ ♥ ♥ ♥ a difficult exercise for the more advanced
♥ ♥ ♥ ♥ ♥ a more difficult exercise for the much more advanced
or athletic participant.

When using equipment to increase the buoyancy and/ or
resistance the number of ♥ equals the intensity of the exercise.

The 🔑 is the teaching point.

This code runs through all our lesson plans and exercise
breakdown sheets.

*Remember all your participants will be at different levels of fitness
and flexibility so it is important to offer progressions for each
exercise throughout. What may be just right for some will be too
easy for others and far too difficult for a few.*

Let your participants choose the level they want to work at.

Warm Up Lesson Plan Shallow – 10 minutes

Exercise	Arms		Time secs	Major Muscles	Progression	🔑
Jog Page 38	Static	Alternate pumping arms	40	Hamstrings	Faster legs	Heels down
Low fwd kicks Page 39	4 fwd 4 back	Double pumping arms	40	Gastroc Soleus	Faster	Soft knees Point toes
Back Toe Tap Page 40	Static	Long double ski arms	40	Glutes Quads Biceps Triceps	Bigger and faster	Soft elbows
Low back kicks Page 41	Static	Alternate arms pushing forward	40	Quads	Faster	Soft knees Soft elbows
Ham curls Page 42	Static	Double opposite side push	40	Quads Lats Oblique's	High heels	Lean toward hands
Small Star jumps Page 43	4 fwd 4 back	Long arms out to surface and hips	40	Abductor / Adductor Deltoids	Bigger and faster	Thighs touch
Mini bounce skis Page 44	4 fwd 4 back	Opposite arms to legs	40	Hams Quads Glutes Biceps Triceps	Longer legs Longer arms	Palm up palm down
Side kick Page 45	Static	Arm pushes away from kick	40	Abductor Adductor Oblique's Lats	Faster	Stretch away from kick
Power jog Page 47	4 fwd 4 back	Power arms	40	Hams Biceps Triceps Core	More power	Squeeze shoulder blades
Wide knee toe tap Page 48	Static	Bring toes to hands	40	Lats Sartorius	Shoulder under	Back straight Abs tight

36

Long back kicks Page 49	Static	Both arms push forward	40	Quads Glutes	Shoulder under	Straight legs Soft knees
Mid high forward kicks Page 50	Static	Clap behind back	40	Hamstring Pectorals	Shoulder under	Back straight Abs tight
Squat jacks Page 51	4 side	Bent elbows to surface and ribs	40	Deltoids Abductor Adductor	Add a tuck	Lead from the elbows
Twists Page 52	Static	Arms opposite direction	40	Oblique's Trapezius	Bounce it	Hips opposite to feet
Sprint Page 82	Static	Breast stroke arms	40	Hamstring Pectorals Trapezius	Increase speed	Full circles

Exercises – Standing Jogging

♥ Standing tall, both feet together on the pool floor, keep the back straight. Raise one knee upwards keeping the foot flat, lower the leg and repeat with the other leg. Ensure the foot returns to the floor and the heel touches the pool bottom. The arms work in opposition to the legs to maintain core stability and can push forwards and backwards in time with the leg movementts.

♥♥ Make the leg change over faster.

♥♥♥ Cardio: Push up through legs, so the body rises out of the water increasing the momentum.

♥♥♥♥ Travel the exercise forwards and backwards.

🔑 **Feet back flat on the floor**

Your own notes:

_____

_____

_____

Low Forward Kicks

♥ Standing tall, raise foot and lower leg upwards with toe softly pointed down towards the pool floor, keeping soft knees, lower leg and repeat on the other side. Arms can push forward, fingers upwards as the leg raises, and pull back down to the hips with fingers pointing to the pool floor as the leg lowers.

♥♥ Make the change over faster.

♥♥♥ Cardio: Push up through legs and bounce as the leg rises, pull the leg down harder and as soon as it touches the floor, bounce the other leg up.

♥♥♥♥ Travel the exercise forwards / backwards.

🔑 **Power back down**

Your own notes:

_____

_____

_____

Alternate Back Toe Tap

♥ Standing tall, tummy muscles engaged, push one leg backwards and tap toes lightly on the floor. Keeping the toes pointed towards the pool floor, pull the leg back into start position and change legs. The arms can alternately push forward in opposition to the legs.

♥♥ Make the change over faster.

♥♥♥ Cardio: Push back through legs, add a mini jump on the changeover of legs, and use double push arms in time with the legs.

🔑 Soft knees

Your own notes:

_____

_____

_____

Low Back Kicks

♥ Standing tall, tummy muscles engaged, push one leg backwards from the hips. Lead the kick from the heel and keep the toes approx. 10 cm from the pool floor. Pull the leg back to start position and change leg. The arms can push backwards with the elbow leading.

♥♥ Make the change over faster

♥♥♥ Cardio: Push back through legs and add a mini jump on the changeover of legs, keep arms in time with the legs.

🔑 **Keep the back straight, lean forward slightly if necessary**

Your own notes:

_____

_____

_____

Pointed Toe Hamstring Curl

♥ Standing tall, bend leg at the knee, keeping hips forward and knees pointing downwards. Raise heel behind as high as possible close to your bottom; point the toes towards the pool floor. Breaststroke arm movements.

♥♥ Make the changeover faster.

♥♥♥ Cardio: Bounce the exercise and increase the momentum. Use power arms.

🔑 **Heels to bottom**

Your own notes:

_____

_____

_____

Small Star Jumps

♥ Start by standing tall and straight with legs hip width apart and arms slightly outstretched to side. Toes facing forwards. Hands must stay under the surface at all times, jump arms and legs back into a standing tall position, making sure thighs meet and hands come back to the hips. Repeat.

♥♥ Increase the speed and power of the arms and legs.

♥♥♥ Cardio: bounce the exercise as legs come together and push apart. Then increase the momentum.

♥♥♥♥ Travel the exercise forwards / backwards.

🔑 **Thighs must meet**

Your own notes:

_____

_____

_____

Mini Bounce Skis

♥ Extend right leg and left arm forward, left leg and right arm backwards, arms fully extended, knees slightly bent. Keep core muscles tight, push upwards off the pool floor change legs and arms while in the upwards push mode, landing softly.

♥♥ Increase speed but keep full extension.

♥♥♥ Add a tuck jump by lifting both knees at the same time towards the chest, and keeping the knees and legs together.

♥♥♥♥ Travel forwards and backwards.

🔑 Feet land at the same time

Your own notes:

_____

_____

_____

Side Kick Crossover Arm

♥ Stand upright, kick one leg out to the side as high as comfortable, with the ankle bone upper most to the pool's surface. Push the arm of the same side with a soft bent elbow across the mid line of the body with fingers upwards. Keep the shoulders fairly square with a slight forward twist of the leading shoulder then change sides.

♥♥ Increase the speed.

♥♥♥ Travel the exercise sideways.

🔑 **Pull leg back to exact centre**

Your own notes:

_____

_____

_____

Crouch Kicks

♥ Lower the body into the water, the standing leg bent, with foot flat on the floor. Extend the other leg outwards. Hop and change legs. Always keep the standing leg bent.

♥♥ Increase the speed and keep the knees soft.

♥♥♥ Hop higher but keep the extended leg under the surface.

♥♥♥♥ Travel forwards and backwards.

🔑 **Hop not kick**

Your own notes:

_____

_____

_____

Power Jog

♥ Standing tall, both feet together on the pool floor, keep the back straight. Jog on the spot by raising knees alternately as high as possible. When putting foot back on the floor make sure the heel makes contact gently with the floor. Pump arms with a bent elbow forwards and backwards keeping hands at waist height. Try to churn up the water.

♥♥ Move faster and bigger.

♥♥♥ Cardio: Push up through legs, so the body rises out of the water increasing the momentum.

♥♥♥♥ Travel the exercise forwards and backwards.

🔑 **Stand tall**

Your own notes:

_____

_____

_____

Wide Knee Ankle Taps

♥ Standing upright, keep both feet together on the pool floor. Extend one knee out to the side, raise foot inwards and forwards and towards standing leg knee. Slightly roll shoulder forward and touch toe with opposite hand. Keep the back straight. The other arm sweeps backwards through the water.

♥♥ Make the changeover of legs faster.

♥♥♥ Cardio: Push up through legs, so standing leg hops as the other knee extends and hand touches opposite foot and increase the momentum.

♥♥♥♥ Travel the exercise forwards and backwards.

🗝 **Roll knee outwards**

Your own notes:

_____

_____

_____

Long Back Kicks

♥ From a standing position with soft knees, push the upper body forward with double arms, fingers pointed to the ceiling while pushing one leg backwards with a flat foot. Extend the leg fully, bend the knee and pull back to starting position, change over legs.

♥♥ Make the change over faster.

♥♥♥ Cardio: bounce the exercise and increase the momentum, with more power on the pushing hands.

♥♥♥♥ Travel the exercise backwards.

🔑 **Lean away from the kick**

Your own notes:

_____

_____

_____

Medium Forward Kick

♥ Standing tall, raise one foot upwards to halfway between the bottom of the pool and the surface. Raise leg from the hip, keep toes pointed upwards on the raise up and lead with the heel of the foot on the lowering down movement. Keep the knee joint soft. Repeat with the other leg. The arms push forwards and backwards, or in and out at the sides.

♥♥ Make the change over faster.

♥♥♥ Cardio: Push up through legs and bounce as the leg rises, pull the leg down harder and as soon as it touches the floor, bounce the other leg up.

♥♥♥♥ Travel the exercise forwards/ backwards.

🔑 Point toes

Your own notes:

_____

_____

_____

Squat Jacks

♥ Standing straight, legs together, arms by your sides. Jump legs out sideways, squat down. Bring elbows together in front of the chest. Jump back in, squeeze thighs together and drop arms back by your sides. Repeat.

♥♥ Increase the speed and power of the outwards and inwards movements.

♥♥♥ Cardio: bounce the exercise and increase the momentum.

♥♥♥♥ Travel the exercise forwards.

🔑 **Thighs must meet**

Your own notes:

_____

_____

_____

Twists

♥ Standing tall to start, bend knees slightly, lift both feet off the floor, keeping knees bent and twist to one side, soft landing, heels touch down on floor. At the same time, swish arms in the opposite direction, keeping arms under the water. Repeat to the other side.

♥♥ Keep shoulders under the surface for the whole exercise.

♥♥♥ Cardio: Push up through legs, and bounce the twist.

♥♥♥♥ Travel the exercise forwards / backwards / sideways.

🔑 Feet off the floor on twist

Your own notes:

_____

_____

_____

Forward Heel Tap

♥ Standing tall, tummy muscles engaged, push one leg forwards and tap heel lightly on the floor, keeping the toes pointed towards the surface. Pull the leg back into start position and change legs. The arms can alternately pull backwards in opposition to the legs.

♥♥ Make the changeover faster.

♥♥♥ Add a knee lift before putting heel on the floor.

Cardio: Not suitable for cardio

🔑 Curl toes to knees

Your own notes:

_____

_____

_____

Knee Raise Flat Foot Back Kick

♥ Standing tall, lift one knee forward up to the chest and then push backwards with a flat foot about knee height, return foot to standing position and repeat with the other leg. Both arms push forward as foot pushes backwards.

♥♥ Make the change over faster.

♥♥♥ Cardio: bounce the exercise and increase the momentum.

♥♥♥♥ Travel the exercise forwards.

🔑 Flat foot

Your own notes:

_____

_____

_____

Rear Cross Kicks

♥ Standing tall, Bend leg at knee, keeping hips forward and knees pointing slightly outwards, raise heel behind as high as possible close to the opposite cheek of your bottom. Breaststroke arm movements.

♥♥ Make the changeover faster.

♥♥♥ Cardio: Bounce the exercise and increase the momentum, use power arms.

♥♥♥♥ Travel the exercise sideways.

🔑 **Hips stay facing forwards**

Your own notes:

_____

_____

_____

Side Rocks

♥ Leaning over to one side, push hand downwards through the water, lean over a bit more and raise the opposite leg out to the other side with a bent knee. Rock over to the other side and repeat.

♥♥ Raise the leg higher in the water and rock over faster.

♥♥♥ Extend the leg outwards into a side kick and bounce the rock over.

♥♥♥♥ Travel the exercise sideways.

🔑 **Lean towards push down hand**

Your own notes:

_____

_____

_____

Side Raisers Cross Pushes

♥ Hips facing forward, raise one leg out to the side as high as possible, toe pointed forward, ankle leading the raise. Push the arm from the same side as the raised leg across the body, finger tips upward keeping hand in the water. Swap sides. Power the leg back to centre, before raising the other one.

♥♥ Make the change over faster.

♥♥♥ Cardio: Bounce the exercise and lean away from the raised leg, and increase the momentum.

♥♥♥♥ Travel the exercise sideways in the direction of the kick.

♥♥♥♥♥ Use one leg and repeat 20 on the one side with power before changing legs.

🔑 **Lean away from kick**

Your own notes:

_____

_____

_____

Rear Ankle Touches

♥ Keeping back straight, standing tall, bend leg at knee, keeping hips forward and knees pointing slightly outwards. Raise heel behind as high as possible and reach behind you. Bring heel up to hand level and change legs.

♥ ♥ Make the change over faster.

♥ ♥ ♥ Cardio: Bounce the exercise and increase the momentum, use power arm.

🔑 **Sweep arms behind**

Your own notes:

_____

_____

_____

Ankle Touches

♥ Keeping back straight, standing tall, bend leg at knee, keeping hips forward and knees pointing slightly outwards. Raise foot to as high as comfortable, slightly roll opposite shoulder forward. Try to bring foot up to hand level and change legs.

♥♥ Make the changeover of arms and legs faster.

♥♥♥ Cardio: Bounce the exercise and increase the momentum, use power arms.

🔑 **Feet to hands**

Your own notes:

_____

_____

_____

Wide Knee Jog

♥ Keeping back straight, standing tall, jogging motion with alternate legs keeping the knees wide and placing the foot back flat on the floor. Pushing the arms forward in opposition to the legs with turned up fingers.

♥♥ Move faster

♥♥♥ Cardio:

Bounce the exercise and increase the momentum. Use power arms and raise the knees wider and higher.

🔑 Knees wide and high

Your own notes:

_____

_____

_____

Jelly Legs

♥ Standing tall, long straight legs, alternately push legs out sideways in small fast movements, pulling them back to the centre. Keep toes facing forwards and the legs straight.

It is not a side kick but a lift and pull.

♥ ♥ Move faster

Not suitable for cardio

🔑 Ankle bone leads

Your own notes:

_____

_____

_____

Interval Training

So now the body is thoroughly warmed up, the synovial fluid in the joints will be warm and ready to allow the joint full range of movement.

The core temperature is a little higher, oxygen levels have increased. The muscles are warm and ready to move freely and the mind is set for some exercise, so now let's explore the main set.

Interval training works best for water fitness sessions. With interval training the participants still work at their own level, it can be as hard or as light as you or your participants make it, but the option to work hard for a short period of time and then recover seems to suit all fitness levels. You can increase or decrease the set time for the "power working" sections, participants can drop back when it suits them, so they put in as much or as little as they wish.

Studies have shown that interval training burns fat faster than the aerobic curve style training. (More about the "aerobic curve" style later.)

As this is the main section of exercise, you should be looking at a minimum of 30 minutes for this section.

What are our intentions?

There are many different styles of intervals; we will concentrate on two of them that work particularly well for water.

Style 1:

Aerobic exercises of 10, 20 or 30 seconds followed by a conditioning exercise of the same time span or greater.

On land the aerobic exercise would be followed by an active rest. Due to thermoregulation in water this is not advisable, so the active rest becomes a conditioning/toning long lever exercise at a lower speed but with increased force. This allows the heart rate to lower, however, the body is still working with long lever resistance exercises which tone and strengthen the muscles.

Style 2:

This is ideal for the overall fitter class, or the class that has been exercising for a long while. But still suitable for all. Just remind the participants that they can lower the effort they put in at any time. It's very important they don't overdo it for their health and safety.

Take 2, 3 or 4 exercises, link them together and keep them all aerobic running for 10, 20 or 30 seconds each. When the group of exercises are completed, allow 30 seconds active rest (pick an active rest exercise at the beginning and use it twice for both sets) then repeat the chosen exercises again, followed by the chosen active rest exercise.

Change the 2, 3 or 4 exercises but stick to the same number and follow the plan and use a different active rest exercise for both sets.

How many sets you use will depend on the number of exercises in each of your sets.

If you use the 30 second option and 4 exercises that's 2 minutes plus 30 seconds active rest so for both sets its 5 minutes. Divide this by the time allocated for your main component to see how many sets you need.

For example, jogging, high kicks, bouncing back kicks and power jumps are all aerobic, followed by jacks as the active rest.

Repeat

Then star jumps, alternate toe touches, rocking horse and alternate sidekicks followed by backward and forward jumps.

Repeat and carry on…

The participants get to do each set twice, the second set will be harder than the first as their energy level will be dropping slightly.

The active rest section means the body is not working so hard aerobically but is still working in a different capacity at a lower heart rate. In this instance it is with more power and force and less speed, i.e. (conditioning). Muscle strength and endurance exercises need to be long lever, using the full range of motion that the participants can safely make. The idea is that the acting muscle group will become slightly fatigued and the participant should be able to tell you which muscles (part of their body) is working at any given exercise, especially after 15 - 20 seconds into it.

When planning the conditioning exercises, make sure there are enough to target each major muscle group of the body for every session. You cannot target upper body one session and lower body the next, as a participant may not attend for consecutive sessions and would miss out.

Interval Training Lesson Plan Shallow – main component 30 minutes

Exercise	Arms legs	Time	Target	Progression	🔑
Rebound Alternate High Kick Page 68	Push up and down by sides	30 secs	Aerobic	Drop shoulders under	Straight legs
Back/Fwd long Jump Page 69	2 arms opposite legs push and pull	30 secs	Abdominal **Pectorals** Traps Biceps Triceps	None	Abs tight
Repeat					
Rebound Alternate Toe touch Page 70	Opposite arm to opposite toe	30 secs	Aerobic	Use both arms	Back straight
Back/Fwd Long Jumps Page 69	2 arms opp legs, push/ pull	30 secs	Abdominal **Pecs** Traps Biceps Triceps	None	1 push, 1 pull
Repeat					
Rocking Horse right leg Page 71	Leg back Push arms forwards	30 secs	Aerobic	More power and Circle	Lean forward
Back/Fwd long jump Page 69	As before	30 secs	Abdominal **Pecs** Traps Biceps Triceps	None	More power
Repeat					
Rocking Horse left leg Page 71	As knee lifts clap behind	30 secs	Aerobic	More power Circle	Knee higher
Bouncing side kicks Page 73	2 arms push away from kick	30 secs	Aerobic	Bounce Higher	More power
Repeat					
Wide star jumps Page 72	Out and in	30 secs	Abductors Adductors	None	Power out

Exercise	Arms legs	Time	Target	Progression	🔑
Tuck Ups Page 874	Wide to hug knees	30 secs	Aerobic	Bounce higher	Back straight
Repeat					
Wide star jumps Page 72	Out and in	30 secs	Abductors Adductors	None	Power out
Bouncing back kick Page 76	Breast Stroke arms	30 secs	Aerobic	Kick faster	Full circles with arms
Repeat					
Jump ups Page 75	Forward / back	30 secs	Abdominal Pecs	None	Abs tight
Leap frogs Page 77	Push hands to inner ankles	30 secs	Aerobic	Gain height	Back straight
Repeat					
Jump Ups Page 75	Arms forwards and back	30 secs	Abdominal Pecs	None	Abs tight
Ski Page 79	Long arms fully extended	30 secs	Aerobic	Bounce	Land feet at same time
Repeat					
Jump ups Page 75	Arms forward/ back	30 secs	Abdominal Pecs	None	Abs tight
Can-can legs Page 92	Circles	30 secs	Aerobic	Kick higher	Toes out
Repeat					
Elbow to knee cross over Page 80	Hands on the surface, opposite elbow to opposite hip	30 secs	Aerobic	Bounce	Keep back straight
Squat kick LEFT leg Page 88	2 x right punches	30 secs	Hamstring	None	Aim to punch centre

Exercise	Variation	Time	Muscle	Intensity	Technique
Repeat					
Ski & tuck Page 81	Extended full range	30 secs	Aerobic	Bounce higher	Both feet land
Squat kick Right leg Page 88	2 x left punches	30 secs	Hamstring	None	Aim for same spot
Repeat					
Sprint Page 82	Running arms	30 secs	Aerobic	Faster	Churn the water
Raiser back kicks RIGHT LEG Page 83	Swing forwards and backwards for balance	30 secs	Hamstring Quads	None	Back straight
Repeat					
Clap kicks Page 84	Clap front and behind	30 secs	Aerobic	Bounce	Back straight
Raiser back kicks Left Leg Page 83	Swing forwards and backwards for balance	30 secs	Hamstrings Quads	None	Return to neutral
Repeat					
Opposite jacks Page 87	Arms in legs out	30 secs	Aerobic	Increase power	Back straight
Wide Leg crosses Page 91	Arms opposite	30 secs	Oblique's Abductors Adductors		Standing knee soft
Repeat					
Squat lift Page 97	Arms push down & pull back	30 secs	Aerobic	Add power	Soft knees
Wide Leg crosses Page 91	Swing arms opposite to kick	30 secs	Oblique's Abductors Adductors		Standing knee soft
Repeat					

Interval Exercises Alternate Leg High Kicks

♥ Standing tall, raise leg upwards with toe pointed to ceiling as in 1ˢᵗ picture, power from the hips. Lower leg and repeat on the other side. Arms can pull back from the elbows as the leg raises and lower to the pool floor as the other leg raises.

♥♥ Make the change over faster and point toe forwards as in 2ⁿᵈ picture.

♥♥♥ Cardio: Push up through legs, and bounce as the leg raises, pull the leg down harder and as soon as it touches the floor, bounce the other leg high.

♥♥♥♥ Travel the exercise forwards.

🔑 **Power the legs down**

Your own notes:

_____

_____

_____

Backward and Forward Long Jumps

♥ From a standing position, tummy engaged swing the upper body forwards until the toes are just touching the floor behind you. Push the arms out in front to initially balance the body. Keep the abs tight, bend the knees slightly, swing upright and carry on pushing through until the top half of your body is laying back, abs tight and just your heels are resting on the floor. Keep the back straight throughout the movements. Aim for a straight line from toes to chin and heels to shoulders every time.

♥♥ Make the exercise harder by increasing the speed, but maintain correct body position at all time.

This is not a cardio exercise.

♥♥♥ Travel the exercise forwards and backwards.

🔑 **Keep body in a straight line**

Your own notes:

_____

_____

_____

Alternate Toe Touch Kicks

♥ From a standing position with soft knees, raise one leg forward, straightening it as it rises, bring foot up to extended opposite hand and touch as close to toe as comfortable. Change legs and arms and repeat.

♥♥ Make the change over faster.

♥♥♥ Cardio: bounce the exercise and increase the momentum.

♥♥♥♥ Travel the exercise forwards.

🔑 Toes up to hands

Your own notes:

_____

_____

_____

Rocking Horse

♥ Start with feet together and standing tall, raise one knee up to the surface, slightly extend both hands forwards with fingers pointing upwards. As the bent leg lowers, rock onto the foot and kick the opposite leg backwards, keeping a soft knee and extending the arms more towards the front.

Try to keep the toes of the back leg pointing towards the pool floor. Lower the back leg and rock onto it while bringing the other knee upwards, and pulling the arms in slightly. Repeat for as long as required and then change legs.

♥♥♥ Increase the power and speed of the exercise.

♥♥♥ Cardio: Bounce the exercise on changeover of legs.

♥♥♥♥ Travel the exercise forwards and backwards.

🔑 **Push and pull the water**

Your own notes:

_____

_____

_____

Wide Star Jumps

♥ Standing tall and straight with arms and legs together, jump arms and legs out to the sides at the same time, then jump arms and legs back to the start position.

♥♥ Increase the speed and power of the outwards and inwards movements for both arms and legs.

♥♥♥ Cardio: bounce the exercise and increase the momentum.

♥♥♥♥ Travel the exercise forwards.

🔑 **Thighs must meet**

Your own notes:

_____

_____

_____

Bouncing Side Kick Double Arms

♥ Hips facing forward push off the floor on the standing leg and kick the other leg out to the side, keeping knees soft and push both arms over to the opposite side away from the kick. Pull arms and legs back sharply and repeat with the other side bouncing on each foot.

♥♥ Make the change over faster.

♥♥♥ Cardio: Bounce the exercise and lean away from the raised leg. Increase the momentum.

♥♥♥♥ Travel the exercise sideways

🔑 **Pull back hard**

Your own notes:

_____

_____

_____

Tuck Up

♥ Start with the arms as wide apart as possible. Power the arms down to the side of the body and knees up towards the chest. Hug the knees to chest, release and then push arms and legs back to the starting position.

♥♥ Increase the speed and power of the inwards pull and outwards push movement.

♥♥♥ Cardio: bounce the exercise upwards on the tuck to increase the momentum.

♥♥♥♥ Travel the exercise forwards.

🔑 **Hug high**

Your own notes:

_____

_____

_____

Jump Ups

♥ Hips facing forward, lower body until the shoulders are fully submerged, balance on tip toes. Push arms out in front of the body, pull tummy in, raise both legs together with slightly bent knees until toes are just under the surface. As the legs rise up, pull the arms backwards until they are level with the hips. As the legs are pushed back to the floor push the arms forward.

♥♥ Make the legs raise faster and power back to the floor.

♥♥♥ Cardio: Bounce the exercise making many repetitive movements and add power to the arm pushes and pulls.

♥♥♥♥ Travel the exercise forwards.

🔑 **Squeeze abs on crunch**

Your own notes:

_____

_____

_____

Bouncing Back Kicks

♥ From a standing position with soft knees, push the upper body forward. Use breast stroke arms while pushing one leg backwards with a flat foot, extend the leg fully, bend the knee and pull back to starting position, change over legs.

♥♥ Make the changeover faster.

♥♥♥ Cardio: bounce the exercise and increase the momentum. Use more arm power with the breast stroke arms.

♥♥♥♥ Travel the exercise backwards, keeping feet flat.

🔑 Lean away from the kick

Your own notes:

_____

_____

_____

Leap Frogs

♥ Stand tall, legs together, elbows slightly out, hands together with fingers touching and parallel to pool floor. Push hands down in the water lowering fingers towards floor and between the legs. Pull the knees up fast and wide. Try to get the knees out of the water and the hands to touch the feet. Push feet back into the standing position.

♥♥ Try to gain more height and faster legs.

♥♥♥ Cardio: Push up through the legs and try to get the chest out of the water Make the movement faster and bigger.

♥♥♥♥ Add travel forwards.

🔑 **Power legs back down**

Your own notes:

_____

_____

_____

Single Leg Forward Kicks

This exercise is a single leg repeater. Start with one side and do a few repetitions before changing sides.

♥ Stand on one leg with a slightly bent leg, kick the other leg upwards, keeping a soft knee, until the toes are just out of the water. Bend the knee and pull the leg back down to starting position. Hands stay facing down.

♥ ♥ Kick the leg faster and power back down to the floor.

♥ ♥ ♥ Cardio: Keep shoulders under the water and work as fast as possible with power, ensuring toes come out of the water and travel in a forwards direction.

♥ ♥ ♥ ♥ Travel the exercise forwards.

🔑 **Keep leg muscles tight**

Your own notes:

_____

_____

_____

Ski

♥ Right leg and left arm forward, fully extended, left leg and right arm backwards, fully extended, core tight, jump and change legs, landing softly. As arm sweeps forward under the water the fingers are raised to give more resistance. As the arm sweeps backwards the fingers are facing the pool floor. Full range of movement.

♥♥ Increase speed but keep full extension.

♥♥♥ Add a tuck jump.

♥♥♥♥ Travel forwards and backwards.

🔑 **Feet land at same time**

Your own notes:

_____

_____

_____

Elbow Cross Over

♥ Standing with the feet hip width apart, soft knees. Keep a straight back. Lift one foot off the floor, keeping the standing leg soft. Bring the knee across the body. Use the opposite arm with a slight shoulder roll to make contact with the knee. The back remains straight and the movement is from the leg not the elbow. Replace lag and repeat with the other side.

♥♥ Raise the knee higher in the water and bring across faster.

♥♥♥♥ Jump up on the standing leg and then pull knee further across the body with speed and power.

⚷ Knees across body

Your own notes:

_____

_____

_____

Ski and Tuck

♥ Right leg and left arm forward, fully extended, left leg and right arm backwards, fully extended, core tight. Jump and raise knees high to chest and change direction of legs, landing softly. As arm sweeps forward under the water the fingers are raised for more resistance and as the arms sweep backwards the fingers are facing the pool floor.

♥♥ Increase speed but keep full extension.

♥♥♥ Travel forwards and backwards.

🔑 Opposite arms to legs

Your own notes:

_____

_____

_____

Sprint

♥ Fast running on the spot. Raise knees as high as comfortable, pump arms with elbows bent as fast as comfortable, try to churn the water.

♥♥ Move faster and make the movements bigger.

♥♥♥ Cardio: Push up through legs, so the body rises out of the water increasing the momentum.

♥♥♥♥ Travel the exercise and change directions multiple times to create drag and turbulence.

🔑 **Churn the water**

Your own notes:

_____

_____

_____

Raiser Kickbacks

♥ Stand feet hip width apart, raise one knee upwards and then power the same leg back straight out behind, keeping a soft knee. Pull the knee back to the start position and repeat 8 – 16 times. Remember to keep the back straight and return to the full upright standing position each time. As the knee raises the arms are behind the body for balance and as the body leans forward and the leg extends the arms reach forward to assist balance.

♥♥ Make the exercise faster

♥♥♥ Cardio: Bounce on the standing leg to increase the momentum, use more arm power.

♥♥♥♥ Travel the exercise by hopping forwards.

🔑 Soft knees

Your own notes:

_____

_____

_____

Clap Kicks

❤ From a standing position with soft knees, raise one leg forward, straightening it as it rises. Bring foot up as close to the water's surface as is personally comfortable. Bring both arms forward and touch hands (clap) under slightly bent knee. Return foot to the floor and repeat with the other leg.

❤❤ Make the change over faster.

❤❤❤ Cardio: Bounce the exercise and increase the momentum.

❤❤❤❤ Travel the exercise forwards.

🔑 **Legs up to hands**

Your own notes:

_____

_____

_____

Lunge Backs

♥♥ Lower body into the water as low as comfortable. Bend one leg avoiding the toes extending past the knees. Stretch the other leg out behind, resting toes on the pool floor. Keep shoulders under the water and change positions, without jumping or bouncing upwards. Keep arms extended to front.

♥♥♥ Increase speed.

🔑 **Stay low**

Your own notes:

_____

_____

_____

Wide Straight Leg Crosses

♥ Keeping the back straight, hips forward and standing with soft knees. Kick one leg across the body, aiming for toes to reach the surface, and toes pointing upwards. Pull back down and repeat with the other side. Swish arms out to the opposite side of the kick.

♥♥ Raise the leg higher in the water and kick across faster.

♥♥♥ Jump on the standing leg and then kick across the body with speed and power.

🔑 Hips forward

Your own notes:

_____

_____

_____

Opposite Jacks

♥ Start standing straight, push arms as wide out to the side as possible. keep legs close together. Power arms inwards so hands and elbows touch, at the same time jump legs outwards as wide as possible. Repeat.

♥ ♥ Increase the speed and power of the inwards pull of the arms and outwards push of the legs.

♥ ♥ ♥ Cardio: Bounce the exercise upwards before the tuck to increase the momentum.

♥ ♥ ♥ ♥ Travel the exercise forwards.

🔑 **Try to get the elbows to touch**

Your own notes:

_____

_____

_____

Squat Kick Alternate

♥ Start with the shoulders under the water, keep the back straight (like in a sitting position). Have both feet on the floor and knees slightly apart. Push up through one leg to standing, while raising the other leg into a forward kick. Pull the kicking leg back down and sit back down in the water. Repeat using the other leg.

♥♥ Increase the height of the kick.

♥♥♥ Cardio: Increase the power of the upward kick, keeping knee soft, and pull back to squat faster.

♥♥♥♥ Travel the exercise forwards by hopping on the kick.

🔑 **Work against the water**

Your own notes:

_____

_____

_____

Power Punch Single Kick

♥ Standing with feet just over hip width apart and the body balanced, tummy engaged. Power one fist forward from the shoulder, keeping the elbows soft and in a straight line. Pull fist back with same amount of power. Kick opposite leg upwards, toe leading in a martial arts style movement, power leg back to the start position and repeat on the other side.

♥♥ Increase the power and speed of the punch and increase the power, speed and height of the kick.

♥♥♥ Cardio: Bounce on both legs for the punch and bounce on the standing leg during the forward kick.

♥♥♥♥ Travel the exercise forwards.

🔑 Muscles tight

Your own notes:

_____

_____

_____

Wide Swings

♥ Standing with feet wider than the hips, abs engaged. Slightly bent knees, lean body forward and arms stretched out wide to the front (to balance the body). Bend the knees further, close legs together, lean backwards and raise feet as far off the floor as possible and arms pushing out behind the body. .Power closed bent legs back to the floor and widen again as they come under the hips.

♥ ♥ Increase the power and speed of the swing upwards and try to get the toes to reach the surface.

♥ ♥ ♥ Cardio: As above but do not allow the legs to touch the floor behind the body, keep a few cm from the pool bottom.

♥ ♥ ♥ ♥ Travel the exercise forwards.

🔑 **Keep abs tight**

Your own notes:

_____

_____

_____

Wide Bent Leg Cross Kicks

♥ Keeping the back straight, hips forward and standing with soft knees, raise one leg with bent knee and kick across the body, pull leg back down and repeat with the other side.

Kick the water across and upwards with the inner side of the foot.

♥♥ Raise the leg higher in the water and kick across faster.

♥♥♥ Jump on the standing leg and then kick across the body with speed and power.

🔑 Soft knee on standing leg

Your own notes:

_____

_____

_____

Can-Can Legs

♥ From a standing position raise one leg straight up towards the surface, then bring it back down and tap your toe, raise the same leg back up to the surface. Repeat a few times and then change legs.

♥♥ Increase the speed.

♥♥♥ Cardio: Bounce the exercise and increase the momentum.

♥♥♥♥ Travel the exercise forwards, turn around and repeat until back in start position.

🔑 **Keep leg muscles engaged**

Your own notes:

_____

_____

_____

Hop Single Side Kick

♥ From a standing position raise one knee and with a soft joint, hop and then kick it out to the side, leaning slightly away from the kick and pushing both arms in the same direction as the leaning body. Pull the leg back in and raise the knee and repeat a few times. Change legs and repeat. Keep the shoulders facing front.

♥♥ Increase the speed.

♥♥♥ Cardio: Bounce the exercise and

Increase the momentum.

♥♥♥♥ Travel sideways on the hop, away from the kick.

♥♥♥♥♥ Travel sideways towards the kick

🔑 **Push away from the kick**

Your own notes:

_____

_____

_____

Swing Kicks Single

♥ Start by standing on one leg, knee slightly bent, lean forward and push arms forward as the other leg kicks out behind in a straight line, heel in line with buttocks, toes pointed down towards the pool floor. Pull the body upright as the leg swings through the water towards the surface in front of you. Control the upwards movement and keep abdominal muscles engaged. Do a few sets before changing legs.

♥♥ Increase the range.

♥♥♥ Cardio: Increase the intensity, speed and range.

♥♥♥♥ Keep shoulders under the water.

🔑 Use power against the water

Your own notes:

_____

_____

_____

Running

♥ Running through the water, ensuring back is straight, knees lift and the foot lands gently on the floor - toe, ball, heel. Travel in all directions. Keep hands under the water and wider than the body.

♥♥ Make the steps bigger.

♥♥♥ Cardio: Increase the intensity, speed and range. Five seconds in one direction, turn to run back through the moving water.

♥♥♥♥ Run forwards and then run backwards, keeping posture correct.

🔑 **Pump the arms getting elbows back**

Your own notes:

_____

_____

_____

Diagonal Kick Single Legs

♥ From an upright position, bring one knee upwards and diagonal, bring opposite elbow to meet it, as you kick the leg out sideways. Push both arms out to the other side. Repeat a few times and change leg.

♥♥ Make the range bigger.

♥♥♥ Cardio: Add a hop on the standing leg.

🔑 Knee across the body

Your own notes:

_____

_____

_____

Squat Wide Lift

❤ Wide leg stance, squat until shoulders are under the water, legs wide with knees bent. Pull the body upright and keeping knee wide pull sole of foot into inner thigh, replace foot back on the pool floor in the start position of a wide squat, repeat with the other leg.

❤ ❤ Squat lower until chin is on water.

❤ ❤ ❤ Try to build up more speed.

❤ ❤ ❤ Do a few reps before changing leg.

Not suitable for cardio

🔑 **Turn knee outwards**

Your own notes:

_____

_____

_____

Power Splash

♥ Shoulders under the water, feet on the floor together, push up through your knees, raise your knees and straighten your legs as they approach the surface. Keep the shoulders under the water at all times and arms in front of you. Aim to kick your hands. Keep your back straight and shoulders over hips.

♥♥ Increase the speed.

♥♥♥ Try to get toes out of the water.

♥♥♥♥ Try to get ankles out of the water.

🔑 **Squeeze abs on lift**

Your own notes:

_____

_____

_____

Skipping

♥ Stand tall, feet together, soft knees and arms out with elbows bent, circle arms as if you're holding a skipping rope, jump over the rope and push up through your legs. Bend your knees to lift feet off the floor.

♥♥ Increase the speed and height of knees.

♥♥♥ Travel forwards.

♥♥♥♥ Reverse arm circles and travel backwards.

🗝 **Keep back straight**

Your own notes:

_____

_____

_____

Star Tuck Star

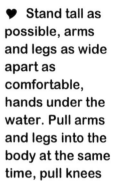

♥ Stand tall as possible, arms and legs as wide apart as comfortable, hands under the water. Pull arms and legs into the body at the same time, pull knees up to chest and hug arms around them. Power back out to the start position.

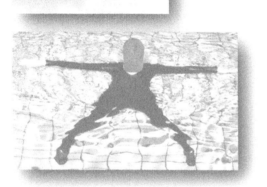

♥♥ Increase the speed and height of knees.

♥♥♥ Travel forwards.

♥♥♥♥ Try to gain height on tuck.

🔑 **Keep back straight**

Your own notes:

_____

_____

_____

Power Backs

♥ From a standing position, tummy engaged swing the upper body forwards and push the legs backwards until the toes are just touching the floor behind you. Push the arms out in front to initially balance the body. Keep the abs tight, bend the knees slightly swing back into a semi crouch position, pulling the arms back to your sides or just behind the body. Push off again swing the upper body forwards again and repeat. Keep the back straight throughout the movements. Aim for a straight line from heels to shoulders every time.

♥♥ Make the exercise harder by increasing the speed, but maintain correct body position at all time.

This is not a cardio exercise.

🔑 **Keep body in a straight line**

Your own notes:

_____

_____

_____

Cossacks

♥ Shoulders under the water then extend one leg forward and out to the side slightly. Rest the heel on the floor with toes turned up. The other leg bends towards the buttocks, with the heel as close as possible and a wide knee. Change over leg positions as fast as possible.

♥♥ Increase the speed.

♥♥♥ Keep the front heel a few centimetres off the floor.

♥♥♥♥ With the heel off the floor, travel forwards.

🔑 Keep back straight, legs wide

Your own notes:

_____

_____

_____

Side to side jump

♥ ♥ Standing upright, abs engaged, jump out to one side keeping hips to the opposite side of feet (aim for a straight line from the ankles up to the shoulders).

Push arms in the opposite direction.

Swing the arms to the opposite side and at the same time swing the body over so the feet touch the floor and you are in a straight line again.

♥ ♥ ♥ Make the jump bigger.

♥ ♥ ♥ ♥ Increase the speed and size.

🔑 Body in a straight line

Your own notes:

_____

_____

_____

Hamstring Curls

♥ Standing upright, abs engaged, raise one foot up towards the buttocks, keep the foot flat and with the knee pointing to the pool floor. Aim to reach the buttocks with the heel. Use breaststroke arms to increase the intensity of the exercise.

♥♥ Increase the speed and size

Note: this exercise is called a hamstring curl as the movements are the same as the land exercise, but due to buoyancy the quads are working on the downward movement not the hamstrings.

🔑 **Knees point to the pool floor**

Your own notes:

_____

_____

_____

Aerobic Curve

Earlier in the handbook we mentioned a different style of training, the aerobic curve. This style is very common in land training and used to be common in water.

- The aerobic curve is exactly what it says it is. You start off with the warm up as usual and you increase the intensity of the exercises gradually as the curve gets higher. At the top of the curve you are exercising at your peak, then the intensity gradually diminishes as the curve reduces, often half way down becoming conditioning exercises. In a land class the cool down and stretch would take place.

Warm up   Aerobic   MSE   Cool down & stretch

If we want to follow this style of teaching for water exercise, we can. There is absolutely nothing wrong with it and this style has been around for many years. But there are some considerations and adjustments for the cooler water temperature that you will need to make.

With the fitness levels of your participants being so varied, it may be hard for the not so fit people to keep up. They may drop back at the first sign of struggling and be unable to recover. Consequently, they can become quickly demotivated in themselves and their ability.

If the participants don't appreciate the amount of power and force they need to execute the conditioning exercises, the exercises can become ineffective and the participants are likely to chill. The cooldown is problematic in the water due to thermoregulation. The participants can cool too quickly to the point of being cold before the stretching. Stretching cold muscles will cause injury and discomfort.

Keeping those 4 points in mind, remind your participants of what they should be doing and how they should be doing it.

For the cool down you can always substitute abdominal work. These exercises are slower but still powerful enough to keep the body warm, while allowing a certain amount of cool down ready for the stretching to follow.

Aerobic Curve lesson Plan – 30 minutes

Exercise	Arms	Time	Target	Progression	🔑
Rocking Horse L leg Page 71	Legs back arms forward	45 secs	❤❤+	Circle round	Lean into the push
Rocking Horse R Leg Page 71	Breast stroke arms	45 secs	❤❤+	Circle in the other direction	upright
Power Jog Page 47	Pump arms alt	45 secs	❤❤+	Add more speed	Core tight
Bounce Ski Page 79	Opposite arm to leg	45 secs	❤❤+	Bigger and higher	Feet land together
Can-Can Legs Page 92	Arms balance body	45 secs	❤❤+		
Rebound Alternate Toe Touch Page 70	Opposite hand to opposite toe	45 secs	❤❤+	Toes pointed forward	Soft landing
Bouncing side kicks Page 73	Arms push away from the kick	45 secs	❤❤+	Kick out higher	Soft knees
Tuck Up Page 74	Wide then hug knees	45 secs	❤❤+	Tuck higher and faster	Back straight
Power Bouncing Back Kicks Page 69	Breast stroke arms	45 secs	❤❤+	Bounce higher & kick faster	Lean forward on kick
Back/Fwd long jumps Page 69	Opposition push and pull	45 secs	❤❤+	Make it bigger	1 push, 1 pull only
Leap Frogs Page 77	Hands to ankles & pull up	45 secs	❤❤+	Jump higher	Back straight
Ski Tuck Page 81	In opposition	45 secs	❤❤+	Power the legs	Stay upright
Sprint Page 82	Pump arms	45 secs	❤❤+	Faster	Back straight
Repeat	+ intensity	10 min	❤❤❤+	Travel	
Repeat the section again	Lowering the intensity	10 mins	❤❤+	Static exercises	Same teaching points

106

Conditioning

Conditioning Lesson Plan – 15 minutes					
Exercise	Arms	Time	Target	Progression	🔑
Hamstring Curls Page 51	Change arms after 30 seconds	1 min	Quads	Increase power	Heels to bottom
Raiser Back Kick Right Leg Page 92	Forwards and back for balance	1 min	Quads Hams	Increase power	Lift knee high kick back straight
Raiser Back Kick Left Leg Page 92	Forwards and bkwd for balance	1 min	Quads Hams	Increase power	Lift knee high kick back straight
Swing Kick Singles Right Leg Page 103	Power forwards and behind	1 min	Quads Hams Pecs Traps	Increase power	Abs tight Knees soft
Swing Kick Singles Left Leg Page 103	Power forwards and behind	1 min	Quads Hams Pecs Traps	Increase power	Abs tight Knees soft
Hop Single Side kick Right Leg Page 102	Push away from the kick	1 min	Abductor Adductor Lats	Increase power	Straight knee facing forward
Hop Single Side kick Left Leg Page 102	Push away from the kick	1 min	Abductor Adductor Lats	Increase power	Standing knee facing forward
Wide Star Jumps Page 81	Surface to sides	1 min	Abductor Adductor	Increase power	Shoulders over hips
Squat Kick Right Leg	front on squat,	1 min	Abductor	Increase	Shoulders

Page 97	pull back to body on kick		Adductor Hams Triceps	power	over hips
Squat Kick Left Leg Page 97	As above	1 min	Abductor Adductor Hams Triceps	Increase power	Shoulder over hips
Back/Fwd long jumps Page 78	opposite to legs, push and pull	1 min	Abs Pecs Traps Biceps Triceps	Increase power	1 push, 1 pull
Jump Ups Page 84	Arm forward and back	1 min	Abs Pecs Traps	Increase power	Squeeze abs
Diagonal Kick Right Leg Page 105	Elbow to knee arms out to sides	1 min	Abductor Adductor Lats Oblique's	Increase power	Knee to elbow
Diagonal Kick Left Leg Page 105	Elbow to knee arms out to sides	1 min	Abductor Adductor Lats Oblique's	Increase power	Back straight
Running Page 103	Steady Pump arms	1 min	Biceps Triceps Quads Hams	Travel	Power not speed

This section is all about long powerful levers, increasing the strength and endurance of the muscles. Using the resistance to enhance the effort needed to target specific muscle groups. The rest of the body needs to be kept moving, suspended or shoulders under the surface works best to maximise the amount of water that the muscle needs to move.

Arms

Our next section is arm only exercises. Most of these exercises will be used with the lower body doing something else, occasionally used on their own if the water is very warm or you want to isolate and target arm muscles specifically. If you choose to isolate the arms for arm work only, then this has to be for a very short time.

For arm exercises to be effective, the shoulder joint should be covered by the water. The hydrostatic pressure can then support the shoulder joint. With more of the arm in the water there is more resistance to increase the strength of these exercises.

Unless the water is very warm, great care should be taken when doing arm exercises only. The exercise before and afterwards should be an all major muscle group powerful exercise, so the body does not cool.

The bigger the hand, the more resistance it creates, so a bunched fist is easier than a flat palm push. But a bunched fist is harder than a slice.

Wide arm exercise will help stabilise the body, keeping the arms closer to the trunk will challenge the core muscles more. Whichever you choose to use, arms in opposition to the legs will create more turbulence and ensure the core remains stable.

The arms do not have to do the same as the legs all the time, try ski legs and star jump arms, speedball arms and ski legs, speedball arms and star jump legs, double forward push arms and ski legs. Or, star jump legs and double forward push arms, star jump legs and speedball arms. You get the idea, just keeps it all moving and working against the resistance.

Warning: For anyone with wrist, knuckle or finger issues. Minimise the resistance of the hand movement by choosing one of the three options below for the safest exercises.

A flat pointed hand with palm facing the pool floor and fingers pointing forwards in a slicing action OR in a pushing forwards and backwards mode.

Or a side to side in a slicing mode is the leading with the thumb then little finger, keeping the palm flat on the water.

For another easier option, have the little finger and thumb slicing with fingertips facing the pool floor, ideal for skis.

Speedball

♥ ♥ Keeping elbows level with waist one hand in front of the other, both hands under the water with palms facing inwards. Roll one hand over the other as fast as you can.

Reverse the roll.

♥ To make it easier bunch the fingers to make a small loose fist.

🔑 **Churn up the water**

Can be used with the following exercises:

_____   _____

_____   _____

_____   _____

Circles

❤ ❤ Keeping the elbows tucked in, close to each side of the body.

The palms facing the pool floor with fingers closed. Rotate the arms from the shoulders in a forwards direction, keeping the lower arm muscles tight.

Then rotate in a backwards direction.

❤ To make it easier keep the elbows in contact with the side of the body and slightly cup the hands.

🔑 **Hands create turbulence**

Can be used with the following exercises:

_____   _____

_____   _____

_____   _____

Breaststroke

♥ ♥ Start with arms stretched forwards, thumbs and first fingers touching and dipped slightly downward. Keeping the hands in the same position, pull down through the water, slightly outwards and then inwards round towards your rib cage. (as if making a circle).

When your wrists reach your rib cage, turn your hands over so the palms are facing up.

♥ To make it easier, make smaller circles.

🔑 **Reach and pull**

Can be used with the following exercises:

_____   _____

_____   _____

_____   _____

Cross Pushes

♥ ♥ Starting with one hand, finger tips towards the surface and held at hip height, push across the body so the hand ends up either in line with or just wide of the opposite shoulder. Keep fingertips upwards as you pull the hand back to start position, repeat with other hand.

♥ To make it easier keep the elbow bent more and do not fully extend.

🔑 **Push the water away**

Can be used with the following exercises:

_____   _____

_____   _____

_____   _____

Double Side Pushes

❤❤ From a wide stance, core tight, finger tips raised, thumbs together, push through the water to the left and then to the right. Aim for full range with a slight twist from the waist and shoulders.

❤ To make it easier keep the elbow bent more and do not fully extend.

🔑 **Push the water away**

Can be used with the following exercises:

_____   _____

_____   _____

_____   _____

Double Forward Push

❤❤ Wide leg stance, bent soft knees, thumbs together and fingers upright push the water forward, keeping the hands in the same position, pull the water towards your chest by bending the elbows and pulling sharply inwards.

❤❤ To make it easier keep the movements smaller.

🔑 **Push the water away**

Can be used with the following exercises;

_____   _____

_____   _____

_____   _____

Single Jabs

❤❤ Keeping a soft elbow and lightly bunched fist, knuckles upwards, power the arm straight forward just under the surface of the water. Turn the hand over (knuckles facing the pool floor) and pull sharply back to chest height. Either complete a few reps with one arm and then change arms, or use alternate arms.

❤ To make it easier keep the elbow bent more and do not fully extend.

🔑 Push the water away

Can be used with the following exercises;

_____   _____

_____   _____

_____   _____

Jack / Star Jump Arms

❤❤ Arms long and straight next to body, palm inwards. Extend arms and keep the hands under the water up to surface in controlled manner and power back to start position.

❤ To make it easier do not

raise the arms so high.

🔑 **Power up and pull down**

Can be used with the following exercises;

_____	_____
_____	_____
_____	_____

Ski Arms

❤❤ Right arm fully stretched forward close to body, fingertips up, left arm extended behind body, finger tips flat. Hands sweep from surface finger tips downwards past body until they have changed position with the other arm.

❤ To make it easier only raise the arms half way, but keep the arms long and straight.

🔑 Sweep through the water

Can be used with the following exercises;

_____   _____

_____   _____

_____   _____

Chest Press

❤ ❤ Hands just out of the water, forearms and elbows pressed together, power arms down and out, back of the hand leading, so elbows remain close to and at waist height, thumbs up. Power elbows back together at chest height.

❤ To make it easier just get the elbows as close together as possible.

🔑 **Squeeze**

Can be used with the following exercises;

_____   _____

_____   _____

_____   _____

Clapping

♥♥ Swing arms forwards, bring palms together (clap). Using the back of the hands, sweep the arms outwards and back behind the body. Keep the hands low and turn palms inwards and touch if possible (clap). Keep shoulders down and relaxed throughout.

♥ To make it easier take hands to just behind the hips.

🔑 **Move the water**

Can be used with the following exercises;

_____   _____

_____   _____

_____   _____

Single Side Push

♥ Leaning slightly over, extend arm, keep a soft elbow and fingers pointed upwards, push out in a straight line and bring the other hand into your hips, fingers pointed downwards. Pull the arm and body back to centre. Bring the arm down to your hips while the other arm gets pushed out fingers pointed upwards.

♥ To make it easier keep the levers short.

🔑 **Fingers up, fingers down**

Can be used with the following exercises;

_____   _____

_____   _____

_____   _____

Pull Backs

♥ ♥ Both arms forward, palms facing pool floor, elbows slightly bent. Pull arms back behind hips but still in line with the body, keep palms facing backwards and return arms to start position. Keep shoulders down and back straight.

♥ To make it easier; slice the water, little finger leading the backward move, thumb leading the upward move.

🔑 **Squeeze the shoulder blades**

Can be used with the following exercises;

_____   _____

_____   _____

_____   _____

Flutter Arms

♥ ♥ Keep the back straight and solid stance. Tuck elbows into your sides, extend forearms forwards and keep wrists and hands tight. With very small powerful movements, flutter up and down from the elbow, keeping forearm straight, as fast as you can. Aim for 15 seconds and build from there. Keep hands in the water throughout.

♥ To make it easier, make softer slightly bigger flutters

🔑 **Keep elbows tight to body**

Can be used with the following exercises;

_____   _____

_____   _____

_____   _____

Sculling

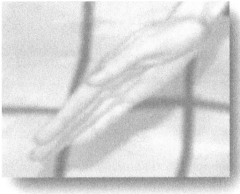

❤❤ Using a very slightly cupped hand, fingers together, thumb uppermost, pushing the water side to side by pushing then turning the hand so the thumb is towards the pool floor.

❤ Change hand position to a loosely clenched fist to decrease the resistance. This is not sufficient for any exercise that requires elevation of the shoulders.

🔑 **Palms lead all moves**

Can be used with the following exercises;

_____   _____

_____   _____

_____   _____

Circuits

A different style of class to shake things up a bit.

Depending on the pool depth, the actual shape and size of the pool, circuits can be fun.

A circuit class is moving around the pool to different stations (areas). If you have limited pieces of equipment this is an ideal class.

It works best if you have some laminated sheets with the exercises on them.

Keep it simple and place one of these sheets at regular intervals around the pool. Make sure you have enough room for 3 or 4 people to exercise at each station.

Dampen the back of the laminated sheet and stick it on to an upright float. Stand another float behind it to keep the pair standing so they are easy for the participants to read.

Suggestion of layout

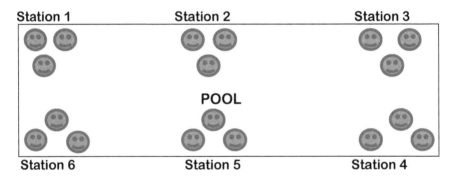

18 class participants, divided into 6 stations, 3 at each station.

If you want to use equipment for the conditioning section, place 3 pieces of equipment at each station. If the pool only has 6 sets of handbuoys place these at station 1 and 5, if you have six noodles place them at Station 3 and 6.

On the warm up your participants can go round the 6 circuits once. For the aerobic and conditioning section, they can go round once or twice. The timing is up to you.

You need to make sure that all the participants are doing what they should be doing, and they have good body position and lots of motivation. You control when the class moves to the next station.

The participants can run to the next station, jump, hop or walk.

You may need to visit each station as quickly as possible to demonstrate an exercise, or to correct someone.

The cards can be used again and changed each week.

Circuit classes can also be held in a line, 3 rows of participants, tey all do the same exercise, the front row rebounds the exercise, the middle row has shoulders under and the back row is suspended. After the exercise again use the circuit cards they front row goes to the back and the other two rows move forward and the exercise is repeated again, and again until all 3 rows have done the 1 exercise in all 3 positions. Then another exercise is used.

The opportunities you can create are endless.

Circuit Lesson Plan						
Station	**1**	**2**	**3**	**4**	**5**	**6**
Warm up	Jog	Back kicks	Wide toe touch	Jacks	Skis	Side kicks
Aerobic	Sprint	High leg kicks	Bounce skis	Power jacks	Knee to elbow cross overs	Rebound alternate toe touches
MSE	Rocking horse	Leg cross overs	Sole touch	Side kicks	Star jumps	Suspended flutter kicks
Ab Work	Crunch	Side to side jumps	Knee tucks	Twists	Forward and back jumps	Pendulum swings
Stretch	Hams	Quads	Oblique	Biceps	Abductor	Shoulders
	Triceps	Pecs	Traps	Upper back	Gastroc	Reach up Breath

Suspended Exercises

These suspended exercises mean the body is literally suspended in the water and not touching the pool floor or the pool sides.

The exercise is executed without any support from an external source.

The participant's centre of gravity (found in the hip area) and centre of buoyancy (found in the chest area) must be aligned to carry out these exercises efficiently.

Many instructors use equipment to help their participants suspend, either because they are not fit enough to balance their body in the water or because they are nervous of having their feet off the floor.

If using suspended exercises in your session, always give an alternative for those who are not confident / strong enough etc. to do them.

Body positioning is very important for the exercise to be effective and to avoid injuries, so it is better that those who are not totally happy with them don't try them. You cannot exercise effectively when you are tense and nervous.

Suspended exercises are easier for your endomorph participants as they have the extra adipose tissue to help them float. Mesomorphs will find suspended exercises increasingly difficult due to their heavier muscle density. (See page 9)

For the body to be able to suspend in water it needs strength, power and speed. These exercises can be quite difficult to master as they involve a lot of limb movement to keep the body above the surface and a considerable amount of core strength to hold the body in the correct position, sometimes both at the same time.

There is a certain amount of buoyancy that will help keep the body up, but the rest of the suspension is down to the actual participant themselves.

These exercises are very effective. They can fit into the aerobic capacity due to the amount of effort the body needs to provide, but they can also fit into the conditioning section as they are repetitive and powerful.

All the suspended exercises shown here are without equipment, so the participant needs to be confident in the water and reasonably physically fit.

High Cross Overs Suspended

♥ ♥ Keeping the back straight, raise both legs towards the water surface, toes pointing upwards. The arms start a sculling action (small forwards, downwards and backwards movements) to keep the head above the water. Without touching the floor, cross one leg over the other keeping one leg straight and the ankle of the bent leg as high up on the thighs as possible, then still without touching the floor change over legs. Avoid putting the foot on the knee joint!

♥ ♥ ♥ Raise the legs higher in the water.

♥ ♥ ♥ ♥ Scull faster and try to get the shoulders elevated out of the water.

🔑 **Keep back straight**

Your own notes:

_____

_____

_____

Suspended Inner Thigh Touches

♥♥ Keeping the back straight, raise both legs towards the water surface, toes pointing upwards. The arms start a sculling action (small forwards, downwards and backwards movements) to keep the head above the water without touching the floor. Bend one knee out to the side and bring the sole of that foot inwards to touch the inner thigh of the other leg. Repeat with the other leg, again without touching the pool floor.

♥♥♥ Raise the legs higher in the water.

♥♥♥♥ Scull faster and try to get the shoulders elevated out of the water.

🔑 **Aim for upper thigh**

Your own notes:

_____

_____

_____

Sole Touches

❤❤ Keeping the back straight, raise both legs towards the water surface, toes pointing upwards and the arms reaching out towards the toes. Pull downwards from the knees so the sole of the feet touch. Widen the arms for balance.

Repeat without touching the floor if possible.

❤❤❤ Use sculling arms.

❤❤❤❤ Scull faster and try to get the shoulders elevated out of the water.

❤❤❤❤❤ Travel forward while feet are still off the floor.

🔑 **Toes and heels to meet**

Your own notes:

_____

_____

_____

Suspended Flutter Kicks

♥ ♥ Keeping the back straight, lean back very slightly. Stretch both legs out and up towards the water surface keeping a soft knee joint, toes pointing forwards. The arms start a sculling action (small forwards, downwards and backwards movements) to keep the head above the water. Kick upwards and downwards in small fast movements, making a splash around your toes. Maintain your balance and try not to travel backwards by increasing the power with your arms.

♥ ♥ ♥ Kick bigger, harder and deeper in the water.

♥ ♥ ♥ ♥ Scull faster and try to get the shoulders elevated out of the water, while still making a splash.

🔑 **Abs tight**

Your own notes:

_____

_____

_____

Heel to Bottom Kicks

♥♥♥ Keeping the back straight, get into a sitting position. Stretch one leg out in front. Keep the knee in line with the hips. With the other leg kick the foot backwards to try to get the heel towards the buttocks. Pull the foot down and forwards until it is straight out in front, repeat with the other leg. Both arms are sculling (small forwards, downwards and backwards movements) to keep the head above the water.

♥♥♥♥ Kick bigger, harder and deeper in the water.

♥♥♥♥♥ Scull faster and try to get the shoulders elevated out of the water.

🔑 **Knee soft on upward kick**

Your own notes:

_____

_____

_____

134

Pendulum Swings

❤❤ Keeping the back straight, stretch out on your side in the water, keeping both legs together and the arm submerged stretched out. Curl up staying on your side, pull yourself into a sitting position and stretch out on the other side, keeping hips facing the pool floor and ceiling (one hip up, the other facing down).

❤❤❤ Make the exercise faster but stay in control.

❤❤❤❤ Keep repetitions to one side, as you pull to sitting, make sure the body is absolutely straight and push back out to the same side you came from. Do a few and then repeat the same amount on the other side.

🔑 Aim for a straight line

Your own notes:

_____

_____

_____

Seated Twists

♥ ♥ With a straight back, abs engaged and in a sitting position, curl knees to chest and push knees over to one side. The arms push in the opposite direction. Bring knees to centre and repeat on other side.

♥ ♥ ♥ Make the exercise faster but stay in control.

♥ ♥ ♥ ♥ Push directly from one side to the other side without stopping in the centre.

♥ ♥ ♥ ♥ ♥ Make all repetitions on one side, as you pull to centre, make sure you are absolutely straight and push back to the same side you came from. Repeat the same amount on the other side.

🔑 **Twist from the waist**

Your own notes:

_____

_____

_____

Cycle Circles

♥♥♥ Keeping the back straight, lie over to one side, curl knees to chest and cycle legs round in circles in a forward direction, driving the water with your heels. Arms can push the water backwards.

Roll over onto the other side and repeat.

♥♥♥♥ Make the exercise faster by speeding up the cycle motion of the legs.

♥♥♥♥♥ Cycle forward for a complete circle, then in the same position flutter kick forwards so you travel in a circle in reverse.

Repeat then roll over and start again.

🔑 **Use the power in your legs**

Your own notes:

_____

_____

_____

137

Knee Tucks Prone

♥♥♥ Laying prone (on your front), shoulders slightly higher than hips and heels, scull with your hands. Keeping the body stable and the back straight, bring both knees forward, keeping the toes pointed to the pool floor, and push back to the start position. Keep the abdominal muscles engaged throughout this exercise.

♥♥♥♥ Bring the knees up higher.

♥♥♥♥♥ Increase the speed, but don't jerk the exercise.

🔑 **Keep bottom slightly below shoulders**

Your own notes:

_____

_____

_____

138

Suspended Wide Toe Touches

♥♥♥ Starting from a sitting position, back straight, stretch legs out in front, keeping the legs close together, abs tight. Point toes to the ceiling, reach forward towards toes without leaning forward then power legs out wide as comfortable, try to touch toes.

Bring legs back in together and return to starting position. Repeat.

♥♥♥♥ Increase the speed.

♥♥♥♥♥ Increase the power and size of the exercise.

🗝 **Thighs squeeze together**

Your own notes:

_____

_____

_____

Suspended Toe Tuck Touch

♥♥♥ Sit in the water, back straight, stretch legs out in front, wide as comfortable, abs tight, point toes to the ceiling. Without leaning forward, power legs out, try to touch toes. Bring legs back in together, raise knees and hug, then return to starting position. Repeat.

♥♥♥♥ Increase the speed.

♥♥♥♥♥ Increase the power and size of the exercise.

🔑 Stay upright

Your own notes:

_____

_____

_____

Suspended Knee Tuck

♥♥♥ Sit upright in the water, keep the back straight and abdominal muscles engaged. Stretch the legs out in front of the body, toes out of the water. Pull the knees up to the chest keeping knees and feet together, and hold with the arms wrapped around the knees and the feet still under the surface of the water. Hold your position, then stretch the legs out forwards again while keeping the knees soft and toes above the surface of the water.

♥♥♥♥ Increase the speed.

♥♥♥♥♥ Increase the power and size of the exercise.

🔑 **Soft knees on extension**

Your own notes:

_____

_____

_____

141

Suspended Cross Over

♥ ♥ ♥ Sit upright in the water, keep the back straight, stretch legs out in front, wide apart, abs tight. Point toes to the ceiling, pull legs back together, crossing one over the other, push back out to start position. On the next cross over make sure the opposite foot is used.

♥ ♥ ♥ ♥ Increase the speed.

♥ ♥ ♥ ♥ ♥ Increase the power and size of the exercise.

🔑 **Lean forward slightly**

Your own notes:

_____

_____

_____

Thigh Squeezers

❤❤❤ Sit upright in the water, keep the back straight, stretch legs out in front, close together, abs tight. Point toes to the ceiling, pull legs wide apart and power back together, squeezing the thighs together as they meet. Repeat.

❤❤❤❤ Increase the speed.

❤❤❤❤❤ Increase the power and size of the exercise.

🔑 **Squeeze**

Your own notes:

_____

_____

_____

Wide Roll Swings

❤ ❤ ❤ ❤ Lie on your back, arms and legs fairly wide, keeping legs absolutely straight. Using your abs, swing the body forward until upright and keep the momentum going until you are fully stretched out on your front. Then swing the legs downwards, keeping the legs straight and wide until you are upright. Keep the momentum going until you are back at the start position.

It is important for the knees NOT to bend at all to avoid lower back injury

❤ ❤ ❤ ❤ ❤ Increase the power and size of the exercise but stay in control.

🔑 **Legs must remain straight and wide**

Your own notes:

_____

_____

_____

Suspended Cycles

♥♥ Sit in the water, keep the back straight, stretch legs out in front close together, abs tight. Point toes forward and cycle. Keep the legs high in the water and drive the heels down in a circular motion. Keep feet submerged at all times.

♥♥♥ Travel forwards.

♥♥♥♥ Increase the speed and use sculling arms to remain on the spot.

♥♥♥♥♥ Add powerful reverse breaststroke arms, increase the power of the legs and try to stay in the same place.

🔑 **Power legs**

Your own notes:

_____

_____

_____

Suspended Skis

♥♥♥ Right leg and left arm extended forward as far as comfortable. Left leg and right arm extended fully backwards, core tight. Sweep through the water changing the position of the legs and the arms. Fingers should push the water, not slice. Keep legs fully extended both front and back and feet off the floor.

♥♥♥♥ Increase speed but keep full extension.

♥♥♥♥♥ Travel forwards.

♥♥♥♥♥♥ Travel backwards.

🔑 **Back leg straight**

Your own notes:

_____

_____

_____

Suspended Running

♥♥ Running through the water, keep the back straight, the feet flat and stay off the pool floor. Pump arms and keep hands slightly curved at finger tips to allow the water to be pulled backwards.

♥♥♥ Raise the knees higher.

♥♥♥♥ Cardio: increase the intensity, speed and range. Five seconds in one direction, turn to run back through the moving water.

♥♥♥♥♥ Change direction of travel quickly causing turbulence.

🔑 **Stay upright**

Your own notes:

_____

_____

_____

Side Leg Raisers

♥ ♥ ♥
Keeping the back straight, stretch out on your side in the water, keeping both legs together and the lower arm stretched out and submerged. Use the upper arm to help balance the body.

Keep abs tight and legs long. Push the bottom leg down towards the pool floor and then control the upward movement. Repeat a few, and then roll to the other side and change legs.

♥ ♥ ♥ ♥ Make the exercise faster but stay in control.

🔑 **Aim for a straight line**

Your own notes:

_____

_____

_____

Crunches

♥♥♥ Lie back in the water, body in a straight line, hips up, toes out of the water. Keep your arms by your side. Using your abdominal muscles, roll up to a sitting position by pushing your bottom towards the pool floor. Roll up as far as you can get, keeping feet out of the water and bringing your arms forward if needed. Lie back down in a slow and controlled manner, keeping hips up and toes out of the water at all times.

♥♥♥♥ Sit up further.

♥♥♥♥♥ Aim for the toes to be above the water surface all the time.

🔑 Use your abs not your neck

Your own notes:

_____

_____

_____

Static Ankle Flicks

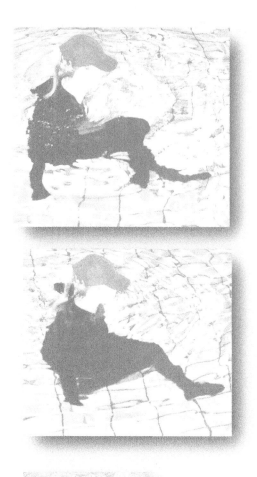

♥ ♥ Sitting upright in the water, knees in line with hips, feet forward from the knees. Use both hands in a paddling motion (trying to move the body forward) Keep feet forward from knees, flick the feet backwards and forwards under the surface of the water, keeping the toes pointed so there are no splashes. Do not let the feet go under your bottom.

♥ ♥ ♥ Make the movement bigger and keep the toes lightly pointed.

♥ ♥ ♥ ♥ Kick harder, paddle faster.

🔑 **Fast and small**

Your own notes:

_____

_____

_____

Raising Cross Overs

❤❤ Keep the back straight and the abs engaged. Cross one ankle over the other then the bottom one over the top one.

Each time there is a cross over try raising your legs a little higher until the toes are just out of the water.

Repeat the process of crossing and lowering the legs until they are just off   the pool floor.

❤❤❤ Make the movements bigger and faster.

🔑 **Keep legs straight**

Your own notes:

_____

_____

_____

Long Leg Flutters

♥ Shoulders under the water, abdominal engaged.

Keep the back straight (ish). Kick small and fast from the hips. Keep the legs as long as possible and keep the knees under the surface.

♥♥ Make the range bigger.

♥♥♥ Cardio: Lower legs until 2cm from the pool floor, then kick hard.

♥♥♥♥ Travel backwards

🔑 **Power legs down**

Your own notes:

_____

_____

_____

Exercise Summary

So by now you know there are many, many exercises. Some fit into a single category of their own, like warm up, aerobic or conditioning. However, most of them fit into all categories. It very much depends on the fitness levels of the participants themselves and depending on the length of lever and intensity used.

Jogging for a fit person can be a warm up, whereas for someone just embarking on an exercise plan it would be aerobic.

That is another reason why the instructor needs to monitor the participants' work level. Tell them what you want - if you're in the warm up, tell them to take it easier. This is just a warm up, so use short lever exercises. If they are pushing themselves too hard, tell them slow down and take it steadily.

Explain that in the aerobic section, you would like them to raise their heart rate a bit more. For the conditioning section, you want long movements with power, real effort and not so much focus on speed.

The suspended exercises are much harder as the body needs to use the resistance and buoyancy movements together to keep the body upright. The centre of gravity and the centre of buoyancy need to stay in alignment for the exercise to be done properly and safely. This is another reason for the instructor to make sure correct body position is maintained at all times.

Being suspended takes much more energy and effort to achieve. Therefore, it is a greater calorie burner but it is not suitable for everyone.

Due to the effort needed for suspended exercises, many of them will increase the heart rate significantly. Some will be purely aerobic in nature, some conditioning, but none of them are suitable for a warm up apart from in deep water sessions with use of an aqua belt. The aqua belt will keep the body higher in the water and the actual effort of the exercises can be reduced.

With travelling exercises in deep water, it's much easier to lean forward, you get there quicker, but the exercise becomes ineffective and strains the lower back.

Exercise adaptions

There will be occasions where you will need a range of adaptions to the exercises; the actual adaptation will depend on the reason why an adaption is needed. Common sense and guidance from the participant as to what is uncomfortable usually are the best guidelines. Avoid causing pain and discomfort. Let the hydrostatic pressure support the joint and reduce fluid build-up if it is an injury. Use the resistance to build up muscle strength.

Exercise	Issue(s)	Exercise Adaptation
Jogging	Hips Knees Ankles Lower back	Use deeper water to lessen the impact OR Walking Stepping Knee raisers
Jogging	Arthritis of the foot, toes or ankle	Use deep water OR Use an aqua belt / noodle for total suspension to keep feet off of the floor
Forward Kicks	Lower back	Keep feet low Small flutters
Hamstring Curls	Knee replacements	Small range OR Toe taps
Ski	Hip Flexors	Small range OR Step back, step forward
Suspended exercises	Not confident in water Pregnant	Use a noodle for support Or adapt so feet can touch the floor adapt so feet stay on the floor
Supine exercises	Vertigo Not confident Pregnant	Use standing exercises Change exercise
Crunches	Not confident in water Pregnant	Jump forward & backwards Change exercise
Abdominal	Pregnant or surgery	Change exercise
Arm work	Shoulders	Within the range No equipment
Jacks	Hips Pregnant	Side step Change exercise
Back Kicks	Lower back	Toe tap
Bouncing	Hips Knees Ankles Lower Back Pregnant	Keep shoulders under the water
Side Kicks	Pregnant	Change exercises

Stretching

The importance of stretching cannot be stressed enough. It's not just something that fills a 5 minute gap at the end of the session.

Stretching improves the muscles flexibility and increases ROM (range of motion) and strength.

It also increases the blood and nutrient supply to the muscles. This helps prevent soreness after a workout.

Water exercise and stretching has its challenges - how to keep the muscles warm enough to stretch them out safely, but this can be done with a little thought.

Obviously all major muscle groups need stretching. As we said before, keep one part of the body moving while stretching other parts, unless the water is exceedingly warm, then you have the luxury of prolonging the stretch and taking it a step further.

Stretching Lesson Plan 5 minutes

30 secs Jogging. Alternate fast and medium temp for 10 secs

All stretches held for 20 – 30 seconds each

Stretch	Movement	Teaching Point
Glutes Page 157	Scull with other arm	Pull up & hug tight
Hamstring Page 158	Sculling arms if no support needed	Curl the toes towards knees Sink low
Hamstring Page 159	Circles with the other arm	Curl toes towards knees Leg straight
Quads Page 160	Pulse	Knees level and pointed to the floor
Triceps Page 161	Lift legs to side and pull back in	Hold high
Triceps Page 162	Small flutter kicks	Elbow to ceiling
Obliques Page 163	Static	Let the hand lead
Latissimus Dorsi Page 164	Static, jog in between sides	Hands leading
Pectoral Page 165	Side step	Squeeze shoulder blades
Trapezius Page 166	Pumping wide legs	Push Forward
Abductors Page 167	Swish arms about	Sink down
Hip Stretch Page 168	Scull	Pull over firmly
Calf stretch Page 169	Breaststroke arms	Put your weight through the back leg
Lower arm Page 170	Jogging	Straight arm
Upper & Mid Back Page 171	Static	Hug tight Pull
Adductor Page 172	Scull	Separate feet
Hip Flexor Page 173	Any arm movement	Hips forward
Bicep Stretch Page 174	Foot tapping	Straight arms
Abdominal Page 175	Static	Support lower back

Glutes Stretch

How: Standing on one leg to support the body, keep this knee soft and balance. Lift other leg up as high as possible, keeping your back straight and your abs tight. Hug the bent leg pulling the knee up towards the shoulder and in towards the chest. Hold tight.

Where: This stretch should be felt at the top of the hamstring on the bent leg and in the buttocks.

How long: Hold 20/30 seconds and change legs.

Stay warm: Hold with one arm (the same side as leg) and scull with the free arm.

🔑 **Pull up and hug tight**

Your own notes:

_____

_____

_____

Hamstring Stretch
Shallow Water

How: Stand upright, feet hip width apart. Bend one leg, use the core muscles to support the body. Stretch the other leg out in front, place the heel on the floor, straighten the leg, and curl the toes up. Lower the body.

Where: Feel the stretch from the back of the knee towards the buttocks.

How long: Hold 20/30 seconds and change legs.

Stay warm: Scull with the free arm(s).

🔑 **Curl the toes towards knees**

Your own notes:

_____

_____

_____

Hamstring Stretch

Holding toes, scull one arm

How: Stand upright, feet hip width apart. Use the core muscles to support the body. Keep the standing knee soft or slightly bent. Stretch the other leg out in front, straighten the leg, and curl the toes upwards towards the knee.
Holding toes is optional.

Where: Feel the stretch from the back of the knee upwards towards   the buttocks.

How long: Hold for 20/30 seconds and change legs.

Stay warm: Circle with the free arm(s).

🔑 **Curl toes towards knee**

Your own notes:

_____

_____

_____

Quad Stretch

How: Standing on the supporting leg, knees close together. Bring one heel up to the bottom, and using the same side arm, hold it close. Bring the stretching leg knee slightly backwards but in line with the other knee.

Where: The stretch will be felt in the middle of the front of the thigh in the bent leg - quadriceps.

How long: Hold each stretch for 20/30 seconds then change legs.

Stay warm: Pulse without pulling on the stretching leg.

🔑 **Knee back & pointed to the floor**

Your own notes:

_____

_____

_____

Triceps Stretch

How: Take one arm straight across the body and with the other arm pull it in close. Avoid holding the elbow joint.

Where: The stretch will be felt in back of the straight arm.

How long: Hold each stretch for 20/30 seconds then change arms.

Stay warm: Lift legs out to the side and back in again to centre, short movements.

🔑 **Hold high**

Your own notes:

_____

_____

_____

Tricep Stretch

How: Standing with feet hip width apart, place one hand up over the shoulder and aim to centre it between the shoulder blades. Use the opposite arm to support it by placing the hand on the triceps. Gently push backwards.

Where: The stretch will be felt in the back of the arm that is raised.

How long: Hold each stretch for 30 seconds then change arms.

Stay warm: Small flutter kicks.

🔑 **Elbow to ceiling**

Your own notes:

_____

_____

_____

Obliques Stretch

How: Standing with feet wider than hips, support one side by placing hand on hips. Raise the other arm overhead and lean over from the hips towards the supporting hand side.

Where: The stretch will be felt in the extended side.

How Long: Hold each stretch for 20/30 seconds then change sides.

Stay Warm: Do one side and then before the other side, add a steady jog.

🔑 **Let the hand lead**

Your own notes:

_____

_____

_____

Latissimus Dorsi Stretch

How: Stand with feet wider than hips to give the body good base support. Reach up straight and extend hand to ceiling. Repeat the other side.

Where: The stretch will be felt in the extended side from the hip area up the side off the back.

How long: Hold each stretch for 20/30 seconds.

Stay warm: Do one side, add a steady jog, and then stretch the other side.

🔑 **Pull up from hip**

Your own notes:

_____

_____

_____

Pectoral Stretch

How: Stand with feet slightly wider than hips, or in a step position. Keep the shoulders low, back and down, take both arms behind the body, clasping hands at lower back height. Squeeze the shoulder blades together and lift the chest.

Where: The stretch will be felt across the front of the chest.

How long: Hold for 20 / 30 seconds.

Stay warm: Small flutter kicks or side steps.

🔑 **Squeeze shoulder blades**

Your own notes:

_____

_____

_____

Trapezius Stretch

How: Standing with feet slightly wider than hips. Keep the shoulders low, back and down, squeeze the elbows together and press.

Where: The stretch will be felt across upper back.

How long: Hold for 20/30 seconds.

Stay warm: pumping legs.

🔑 **Push forward**

Your own notes:

_____

_____

_____

Abductor Stretch

How: Stand with feet wide apart. Lower the body into the water by bending one knee and straighten the other leg. Keep the feet as wide apart as possible and toes facing forward.

Where: The stretch will be felt in the inner thighs.

How long: Hold for 20/30 seconds and change legs.

Stay warm: Swish arms backwards and forwards.

🔑 **Sink down**

Your own notes:

_____

_____

_____

Hip Stretch

How: Standing on one leg to support the body, keep this knee soft and balance.

Lift other leg up as high as possible, keeping your back straight and your abs tight. Pull the bent leg across the body by holding with same side hand, either under the back of the thigh or across the shin. Avoid the knee joint. Hold tight.

Where: This stretch should be felt in the hip area and side of the buttocks.

How long: Hold 20/30 seconds and change legs.

Stay warm: Scull with the free arm.

🔑 **Pull over firmly**

Your own notes:

_____

_____

_____

168

Gastrocnemius (Calf) Stretch

How: Start by standing feet together hip width apart, step back with one leg, place this foot in a straight line and push the heel down to the floor, keeping the back leg straight. Push your hips forward. Bend the front leg to gain a more effective stretch.

Where: This stretch should be felt in the centre of the calf area of the straight leg.

How long: Hold 20/30 seconds and change legs.

Stay warm: Breaststroke arms.

🔑 **Put your weight on the back leg**

Your own notes:

_____

_____

_____

Lower Arm

How: Stretch one arm out in front, fingers pointing to the ceiling, palm facing forward, hand at right angles to the arm. With the other hand support the fingers and push back gently.

Where: This stretch should be felt in fingers and lower arm.

How long: Hold 20/30 seconds.

Stay warm: Jogging.

🔑 **Straight arm**

Your own notes:

_____

_____

_____

Upper and Mid Back Stretch

How: Stand just over hip width apart. Curl spine over forwards, bring shoulders together as far as possible in the front - either wrap your arms around your body like a hug and squeeze, or cross arms, opposite hands on opposite shoulders and pull, opening up the upper back.

Where: This stretch should be felt in upper and mid back.

How long: Hold 20/30 seconds.

Stay warm: Static

🔑 **Hug tight**

Your own notes:

_____

_____

_____

Adductor Stretch

How: Sitting in the water, stretch legs out in front of you, toes pointed upwards. Cross one leg over the other at thigh height and avoid crossing on the knee joint. Try to separate the feet, while keeping legs long and straight. Swap over legs.

Where: This stretch should be felt in outer upper thigh.

How long: Hold 20/30 seconds and change over legs.

Stay warm: Sculling arms to keep above the surface.

🔑 **Separate feet**

Your own notes:

_____
_____
_____

Hip Flexor Stretch

How: Stand in the water, feet together. Take one leg back behind the body in a straight line, just the toes of the rear foot on the floor. Push down onto the toes while pushing your hip forward.

Where: This stretch should be felt high at the very top and in the front of the leg.

How long: Hold 20/30 seconds and change over legs.

Stay warm: Alternate pushing arms.

🔑 **Hips forward**

Your own notes:

_____

_____

_____

Bicep / Deltoid Stretch

How: Stand tall in the water, feet hip width apart. Take both arms back behind the body, clasp fingers together and turn the palms to face outwards or downwards, keeping the arms extended.

Where: This stretch should be felt from shoulder to elbow on the front of both arms.

How long: Hold 20/30 seconds.

Stay warm: Foot tapping.

🔑 Straight arms

Your own notes:

_____

_____

_____

Abdominal Stretch

How: Stand tall in the water, feet hip width apart. Place hands on hips to support the lower back. Engage the abdominal muscles, push hips forwards and lean back.

Where: This stretch should be felt down the centre of the trunk and into the top of the legs.

How long: Hold 30 seconds.

Stay warm: Static

🔑 **Support lower back**

Your own notes:

_____

_____

_____

Finale Stretch

How: With feet hip width apart, take a deep breath in whilst raising both arms high above the head until fingers touch. Pull upwards from the hips. Breathe out forcefully as the arms lower in a wide opening movement.

Where: This stretch should be in all muscle groups.

How long: Hold in breath for as long as comfortable.

Stay warm: Static.

🔑 **Deep breath**

Your own notes:

_____

_____

_____

Deep Water

Is deep water any different from shallow water, apart from the fact that you cannot touch the floor?

The answer is yes, deep water is a lot different from shallow water as some of the shallow exercises will work, but many don't.

Any rebound exercises that you can do in shallow cannot be transferred to the deep, as there is no pool floor to rebound off.

Single leg exercises are much harder in the deep, as it is harder to keep proper alignment.

More importantly, there are a couple of major differences.

In deep water, more of the body is exposed to the effect of the hydrostatic pressure; the chest area is covered with water like many suspended exercises. This could cause a problem with any asthmatics, COPD sufferers or anyone who has just got over a bad cold or chest infection. The pressure could also affect any person who is used to shallow breathing, either through a medical reason, habit or stress. The intercostal muscles will have to work harder to expand against the hydrostatic pressure.

There is also a greater risk of drowning for weak swimmers. some of whom think it's acceptable to be in the deep water as they have an aqua belt. The belts are *not* lifesavers. The clips have been known to pop open, leaving the participant sinking under the water. ***This is not a session for weak and non-swimmers.***

The main notable difference is that the centre of gravity and the centre of buoyancy shift when the feet are not in contact with the floor. This can cause poor body position and bad muscle alignment, especially if the core muscles are not as strong as they might be.

A deep water class has greater water movement, as more of the body's surface area is covered by the water, and consequently more water has to move each time a limb or body moves. Keeping correct body alignment is an extra challenge in several ways.

It is essential that all deep water exercises are balanced, so the core remains tight, body positioning is correct, especially when travelling.

177

The deep is perfect for allowing long body alignment that cannot be achieved in shallow water, for people of any height.

For participants not used to deep water exercise, extra care must be taken when changing exercises or changing direction. The centre of gravity and centre of buoyancy must remain aligned to prevent muscle strain, especially in the lower back.

Look out for participants who lean forward when travelling in a forward direction, or lean back when travelling backwards. This is not good body alignment.

Aqua Belts

The correct wearing of an aqua belt is advised unless the participants are very fit, confident swimmers and used to deep water exercises.

Although some participants may be too large for the belts, this will not cause a problem if they are confident in deep water, as their adipose tissue will help to keep them above the water.

The aqua belt is designed to lift the body in the water, allowing for free movement of the limbs and to aid the body's natural buoyancy. As we know, each body has its own level of buoyancy so some alteration may need to be made.

There are many different belts for sale, all made from different materials and all at different prices. Budget is a main concern for all pool operators and instructors. Do have a look around and compare prices. Belts are a major investment, especially if you have big classes.

The ideal belt needs to be fairly mouldable to fit snugly around the participant. If it is too hard, it will not fit and will ride up to, or over the participant's chest. This will restrict breathing and cause friction on the inner arm. If it is too soft, the belt will split due to the number of times the size is altered by different participants.

Some deep water enthusiasts will have their own personal belt. Once the size has been set for them, no adjustments are needed, so the belt lasts longer.

The majority of participants will wear the belt with the clip at the front and the belt around the back. The waist strap must cover the wings of the belt, otherwise they will stick out and rub the inner arms and generally get in the way of the exercises. Unless the belt has been designed with smaller wings then the strap remains on the inside.

The belt should fit snugly around the waist, tight enough not to ride up under the chest, but not too tight so the participant is unable to breathe or feels uncomfortable.

The buoyancy test: Ask the participant to hang in the water vertically, proper body alignment with shoulders back, bottom tucked under, ears, shoulders, hips and ankle in line. The body should not tip forward a great deal.

If the participant tips forward, then advise them to turn the belt around, and try the buoyancy test again. Repeat until the most stable position is found.

How to Fit an Aqua Belt

An aqua belt

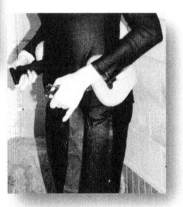

Feed belt around the body with the buckle in front.

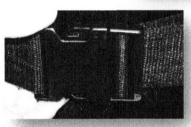

Push the pronged end of the clip into the other side and push hard enough until you hear the 'click'.

Tighten the straps for a snug fit.

Belt connected properly.

For all new participants do a buoyancy test before the warm up the buoyancy test: Page 179

Deep Water Session

With the deep water, the warm up has all the same priorities as any other warm up. That is, to warm up the body, warm up the muscles; slightly increase core temperature; increase the fluidity of the synovial fluid in the joints; slightly increase the heart rate; increase the oxygen levels to the muscle groups; and allow the mind to focus on what the body is doing rather than what is going to happen later in the day or tomorrow.

Again the warm up is anything from 8 to 15 minutes, depending on the fitness level of the participants. The rest of the session is best delivered as interval training. The participants will determine their own speed for travelling. Mix static exercises and travelling, so the fastest participants can keep exercising while others are still on the move.

More of the body is submerged, so the exercises are going to be more challenging (there is more of the body to move through the water. Also more of the skin is covered in colder water, so movement is the key to keeping warm in the deep.

In deep water, the law of action and reaction becomes more important - to move the body forward the water needs to be pushed behind the body; to move the body backwards the water needs to be pushed forwards. As more of the body is submerged there is more drag on the body and the eddy currents become bigger. In addition, more turbulence is created due to the volume of water being moved. The resistance is greater due to a more submerged body parts. So the deep water can make for a very challenging workout.

The deep is also a good time for using buoyancy resisted moves. The downward movement has no restriction, so provided the feet are kept flat a greater surface area is available to work against the buoyancy.

- Keep warm
- Keep correct body alignment
- Wear an aqua belt unless a very fit, confident swimmer and used to deep water exercises
- Opposite arm and opposite leg exercises for core stability
- Be aware of centre of gravity and centre of buoyancy alignment at all times

- Small lever exercises mixed with power moves
- Travel the exercises
- Forwards, backwards, sideways
- Think action and reaction
- Create turbulence
- Use direction changes
- Mix static exercises and travelling exercises
- Make use the deep water, long body, long leg exercises

Deep water Lesson Plan 45 minutes

Exercise	Travel length	Arms	Time	Major Muscles	Progression	TP 🔎
Warm Up			8 - 10m			
Jogging Page 187	Static	B Stroke	1 m	Hams Pectoral	At own speed	Elbow push back
Flutters Page 188	Bwd	Scull	1 m	Tibialis anterior Gastroc	Faster	Power up
Ankle Taps Page 189	Static	Opp to legs	45s	Adduct Sartorius	Wider	Long legs
Jogging Page 187	Fwd	Alt pumps	1 m	Ham string	Faster	Elbow push back
Rear Taps Page 190	Static	Reach behind	45 s	Quads. Lats.	More power	Stay straight
Twists Page 191	Static	Opposit e side	45 s	Obliques	Roll knees over	Twist
Thigh Touch Page 192	Fwd	B Stroke	1 m	Adds Hams Biceps Triceps	Wider	Aim for inner thigh
Low forward Kicks Page 193	Static	Double ski	45 s	Hams Biceps Triceps	Faster	Legs under hips
Cycles Page 194	Fwd	B Stroke	1 m	Gastroc. Tibialis anterior	Bigger moves	Circle with heels
Interval Section			30-32 min			
Deep Skis Page 195	Fwd	Palms push	1 m	Hamstring Quads. Biceps Triceps	More power	Long back leg
Flutters Page 188	Bwd	No arms	1 m	Tibialis anterior	Small and fast	Power legs

183

(R) Leg Swings Page 200	Static	Extend	45 s	Hamstring Quads. Core	More power	Keep upper body stable
(L) Leg Swings Page 200	Static	Extend	45 s	Hamstring Quads Core	More power	As above
Deep Skis Page 195	Fwd	Opp	1 m	Hamstring Quads. Biceps Triceps	More power	Push forward
Jogging Page 187	Fwd	Breast Stroke	1 min	Hamstring Pectorals	Inc speed	Abs engage
Thigh Touches Page 192	Static power	Power pull downs	15 H 15 E x 4	Deltoids Lats.	Chest out	Down hard Easy up
Cycles Page 194	Fwd	Breast Stroke	1 m	Gastroc. Tibialis Anterior Pectorals	Power arms	Drive heels down
Jacks Opposite Page 201	Static	Arms in, legs out	1 m	Abductor Adductor	Inc range	Thighs touch
Cycles Page 194	Fwd	Breast Stroke	1 m	Gastroc. T. Anterior Pectorals	Speed	Back straight
Flutters Page 188	Bwd	Scoop arms	1 m	T. anterior Gastroc.	More power	Soft knees
Jogging Page 187	Static	Alt pump	1 m	Hamstring Pectorals	Knees up	Steady rhythm
Vertical Flutters Page 211	Static	Scull	30 s	Quads. Hamstring Core	Inc speed	Feet under bottom
Elevating Flutters Page 205	Static Power up X 2	Sculling hard /easy	10H 20E	Quads Hamstring Core	Raise higher	Feet under bottom
High Kicks Page 203	Fwd	Swing opp	1 m	Hamstring Core	Touch toes	Remain upright
Long Power Tucks Page 204	Static	Hug and extend	1 m	Abductor Adductor Abs. Trapezius	Inc. power and speed	Back long

184

Deep Skis Page 195	Fwd	Opposite	1 m	Hamstring Quads. Biceps Triceps	More speed	Long back leg
Deep S195 Page 207	Bwd	Use palms to push	1m	Hamstring Quads. Biceps Triceps	More power	Push water forward
Long Flutters Page 202	Static	Sculling	1 m	Abs. Hamstring	Kick deeper	From the hips
As above	Lower ing	Sculling	1 m	Abs. Hamstring	Deeper kicks	Lower slowly
Tuck Splash Page 206	Static	Hug	1 m	Abs. Hip Flexors	More speed	Soft knees
Jogging Page 187	Fwd	Double pump	1 m	Hamstring Pectorals	High knees	Back straight
Jogging Page 187	Bwd	Scoop	1 m	Hamstring Lats.	Wider scoop	Push forward
Power Soles Page 213	Static	Power down	1 m	Adductor Quads. Sartorius	Soles of feet touch	Down and out
Power Soles Page 213	Fwd	Double pull backs	1 m	Adductor Quads. Pecs Sartorius	More power	Pull
Thigh Squeeze Page 143	Static	Pull Down	1 m	Adductor Abductor	More Power	Thighs Tight
Side Scoops Page 207	Travel left	Scoop	1 m	Adductor Abductor	More Power	Thighs meet
Side Scoops Page 207	Travel Right	Scoop	1 m	Adductor Abductor	More Power	Thighs meet
High Kicks Page 203	Static	Touch opposite toe	1 m	Hamstring	Faster	Power down
Ex Heel Flicks Page 209	Travel fwds	B Stroke	1 m	Pecs Hams Gastroc.	More power	Power the kick down

185

Ex Heel Flicks Page 209	Travel bwd	Scoop arms	1 m	Hams Gastroc. Lats.	Bigger arms	Push water fwd
Ab work			3.5m			
Crunch Page 149	Static	Reach for toes	30 s	Abs	Feet out	Toes on surface
Vertical Crunch Page 210	Static	Stabilise	1 m	Abs Adductor Abductor	More power	Abs tight
Curl Twists Page 212	Static	Opposite	30 s	Abs Obliques	Slow and in control	Curl
Pend. Swings Page 135	Static	Opposite	1 m	Obliques	More power	Straight line
Tuck Ext Page 220	Static	Pull down	30 s	Abs	Increase speed	Power
Stretch			4 m			
Abds Page 222	Static	Scull	20 s	Abductor		Scull
Adds Page 223	Static	Scull	20 s	Adductor		Feet apart
Quads Page 224	Static	Scull	20 s	Quads		Hips Fwd
Hams. Page 225	Static	Scull	20 s	Hamstring		Curl toes
Gastroc. Page 226	Static	Wide arms	20 s	Gastroc. Soleus		Heel down
Pecs Page 227	Static/ Cycle	Behind body	20 s	Pectorals		Pull
Biceps Page 228	Thigh pulls	Behind body	20 s	Biceps		Palms out
Triceps Page 229	Tread water	Across chest	20 s	Triceps		Pull arms in
Abs Page 230	Static	Down to floor	20 s	Abs		Long body
Hips Page 231	Static	Scull	20 s	Hips		Knee down
Lats Page 232	Static thigh pulls	Above head	20 s	Lat. Dorsi		Grow taller
Traps Page 233	Jog	Around body	20 s	Trapezius		Hug

Deep Water Exercises

Deep Jogging

♥♥♥ Raise the right knee and bring the left elbow forward at the same time. The left knee is pushed backwards with a flat foot under the body. The body travels forwards as the water is pushed behind the body. Keep the feet flat throughout.

♥♥♥♥ Increase speed and push the leg downwards keeping a soft knee.

♥♥♥♥♥ Travel Backwards and push the water forwards.

♥♥♥♥♥♥ Travel 4 forwards and 4 backwards.

🔑 **Elbows push back**

Your own notes:

_____

_____

_____

Deep Reverse Flutter Kicks

❤❤❤ Sit upright, back straight and abs engaged. Legs forward under the surface. Pull the one foot back under the body getting the heel as close to the buttocks as possible. Then kick that leg back to the start position with power whilst bringing the other foot back under the body. Travel backwards with sculling arms.

❤❤❤❤ Increase speed and power but keep a soft knee.

❤❤❤❤❤ No arm movement.

❤❤❤❤❤❤ Scull hard and try to keep the body from travelling backwards.

🔑 Power upwards

Your own notes:

_____

_____

_____

Deep Ankle Taps

❤❤❤ Long body hanging in the water. Legs down and feet pointing to the floor. Raise one knee upwards and out to the side, while the other leg widens a little to stabilise the body. Use opposite hand to touch the ankle, remain upright. As the legs change over, use the hand not touching the ankle to sweep the water back behind the body.

❤❤❤❤ Increase speed and power.

❤❤❤❤❤ Travel forwards using the sweeping hand to push the water behind the body.

🔑 **Long body**

Your own notes:

_____

_____

_____

Deep Rear Foot Taps

♥♥♥ With a long straight body hanging in the water. Keep the core muscles tight and proper alignment. Raise one foot behind the body, keeping the other leg long and straight.

Keeping the shoulders back and down, reach behind the body with the opposite arm and touch the foot. The other arm pushes out to the side to balance the body.

♥♥♥♥ Increase speed and power.

🔑 **Stay upright**

Your own notes:

_____

_____

_____

Deep Twists

❤❤❤ Bend knees a little while keeping the back straight and push over to one side of the body, while hands push to the opposite side. Bring knees back to centre and push to the other side.

❤❤❤❤ Increase speed and power.

❤❤❤❤❤ Roll the knees over to the side further, until hip is close to the surface, then roll the knees over to the other side.

🔑 Twist from waist

Your own notes:

_____

_____

_____

Deep Inner Thigh Touches

♥♥ Long body, feet under hips pointing to pool floor, swing one leg out to the side. Keeping one leg long, pull the other foot in towards the inner thigh, scull or circle with wide arms and change legs.

♥♥♥ Increase speed and power.

♥♥♥♥ Push the straight leg out wider and aim to touch the inner thigh.

♥♥♥♥♥ Use breast stroke arms to travel forwards, while maintaining a straight back and long body.

♥♥♥♥♥♥ Use powerful pull down arms to raise the shoulders out of the water

🔑 Touch inner thigh

Your own notes:

_____

_____

_____

Deep Low kicks

♥ ♥ Long body, abs pulled in, bottom tucked under. From the hip, kick forward with pointed toes and pull leg back straight. Use alternate legs. Scull to maintain static position.

♥ ♥ ♥ Raising the legs slightly, keep kicking in a raising and lowering action.

♥ ♥ ♥ ♥ Increase the speed.

♥ ♥ ♥ ♥ ♥ Travel forward with breast stroke arms.

♥ ♥ ♥ ♥ ♥ Travel backwards with long double push arms.

♥ ♥ ♥ ♥ ♥ ♥ Kick furiously and elevate the body.

🔑 **Long legs**

Your own notes:

_____

_____

_____

Cycles

♥♥ Maintain a straight back at all times. Extend one leg forward, drive the heel downwards in a circular motion and pull the water under the body with the heel. Repeat with the other leg and cycle. Sculling arms.

♥♥♥ Increase the speed and motion.

♥♥♥♥ Use breaststroke arms to travel forwards.

♥♥♥♥♥ Use reverse breaststroke arms to remain static.

🔑 **Drive heels round in circles**

Your own notes:

_____

_____

_____

Deep Ski

❤❤ Long body, extend the right leg and left arm forwards, the left leg and right arm backwards like doing the splits. Use full range of motion, and then sweep both arms and legs in the opposite direction while remaining upright.

❤❤❤ Increase the speed and motion.

❤❤❤❤ Increase the power of the backward sweep to travel forwards.

❤❤❤❤❤ Increase the power of the forward sweep to travel backwards.

🔑 **Straight back leg**

Your own notes:

_____

_____

_____

Deep Ski Double Arms

❤❤ As with a traditional ski, the legs extend forward and backwards as long as possible.

The arms change to both in front of the body and then both behind.

When the legs change positions, the arms change at the same time. Keep the hands under the water.

❤❤❤ Increase the speed and motion.

🔑 **Straight back leg**

Your own notes:

_____

_____

_____

196

Ski Tuck

♥♥♥ Long body, extend the right leg and left arm forwards, the left leg and right arm backwards like doing the splits. Use full range of motion, and then sweep both arms and legs in the opposite direction while remaining upright.

♥♥♥♥ Increase the speed and motion of the legs and arms.

♥♥♥♥♥ Try to increase the power of the backward sweep to travel forwards.

♥♥♥♥♥♥ Increase the power of the forward sweep to travel backwards.

🔑 Knees up high

Your own notes:

_____

_____

_____

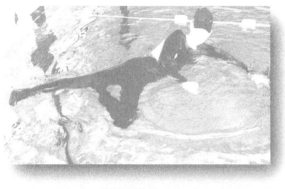

Horizontal Thigh Touch

♥ ♥ Body in a straight horizontal line, stretch both legs out as close to the surface as possible. Keep the upper leg perfectly still; power the lower leg down towards the pool floor, keeping it straight. When the legs is at its lowest, bend from the knee and use the sole of the foot to touch the inner thigh, lower the foot back to the start position. After a few reps roll over to the other side and repeat.

♥ ♥ ♥ When the sole has made contact with the top leg, straighten the leg and pull the whole leg back to the top leg and repeat.

Not suitable for cardio

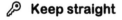 **Keep straight**

Your own notes:

_____

_____

_____

Crocodile Snaps

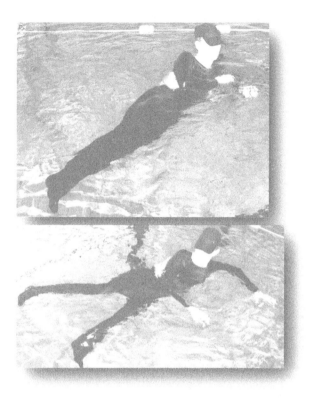

♥ ♥ In a straight horizontal line, stretch both legs out as close to the surface as possible. Keep the upper leg perfectly still, power the lower leg down towards the pool floor, keeping it straight. Control the upwards motion of the lower leg until it meets the top leg and repeat. Roll over so the bottom leg is now on the top and repeat.

♥ ♥ ♥ Increase the power.

Not suitable for cardio

🔑 **Upper shoulder high**

Your own notes:

_____

_____

_____

Deep Leg Swings

♥♥♥ Sit upright in the water. Bend one leg at the knee, keeping the foot under the body to stabilise it. With the other leg, keeping it long and tight swing the leg forwards and backwards from the hip.

Use the arms to stabilise the body by extending out to the side. Repeat a few times and change legs.

♥♥♥♥ Increase the range and power.

🔑 Keep the upper body stable

Your own notes:

_____

_____

_____

200

Jacks in Opposition

♥♥♥ Long body, abs pulled in, back straight and bottom tucked under. Raise the arms in a controlled manner to the surface, keeping thighs together. Power arms back down to the sides while powering legs out as wide as comfortable. Power legs back in so thighs touch and arms return to the surface.

♥♥♥♥ Increase power and speed.

♥♥♥♥♥ Take arms behind the body to touch, then bring them back in front to touch for the next repetition and alternate.

🔑 **Power the legs together**

Your own notes:

_____

_____

_____

Long Leg Flutters

❤❤ Start with a long straight vertical body.

Shoulders, hips and ankles in a straight line.

Keep feet under the trunk and make small fast kick, with toes softly pointing to pool floor. Scull with the arms to remain in the same position.

❤❤❤ Increase the speed.

❤❤❤❤ Increase the power, scull hard and elevate shoulders out of the water for 10 secs, slow it down to recover for 20 secs and repeat.

🔑 **Keep feet under bottom**

Your own notes:

_____

_____

_____

High Kicks

♥♥♥ Keeping body straight kick one leg up towards the surface and pull back down hard. Keep toes lightly pointing towards the surface. Aim to keep the other leg as straight as possible under the body.

Opposite arm swings forward, while same side arm swings slightly backward to maintain balance. Change legs.

♥♥♥♥ Increase speed but keep full extension.

♥♥♥♥♥ Touch toes and travel forwards.

🔑 Upright trunk

Your own notes:

_____

_____

_____

Long Power Tucks

♥♥♥ Sit upright in the water with a straight back, tuck knees up to chest and bring arms around the knees to hug them lightly. In one move, extend both the arms downwards; keep the elbows soft, and the legs downwards and outwards. Keep the feet flat. Pull the legs upwards and together and bring the arms back around the knees for a hug. Repeat.

♥♥♥♥ Increase power and speed.

🔑 **Keep back straight**

Your own notes:

_____

_____

_____

Elevating Long Leg Flutters

♥♥♥ Shoulders, hips and ankles in line; abdominal muscles engaged throughout. Start with sculling by the hips, small alternate kicks, gradually raising legs higher and sculling arms wider, until the hands and the feet are just under the surface.

Repeat action but lower the legs back to under the body.

♥♥♥ Kick deeper.

♥♥♥♥♥ Kick deeper and faster and bring legs up slower.

♥♥♥♥♥♥ Scull faster and raise shoulders out of water.

🔑 Kick from the hips

Your own notes:

_____

_____

_____

Long Tuck Splash

♥♥♥ Start with a straight body, with long legs and feet pointing to the pool floor.

Pull both knees up to the chest and then push both legs out in front of the body in line with the surface of the water. Using the feet to push the water away.

Keeping the abs engaged, the back straight throughout and soft knees, pull the knees back to the chest and lower to the pool floor.

♥♥♥♥ Increase the speed.

♥♥♥♥♥ Raise the legs higher.

🔑 **Back straight**

Your own notes:

_____

_____

_____

Side Scoops

♥♥♥ Long body hanging in the water keeping ankles under knees, knees under hips, hips under shoulders. Bend and stretch one leg out to the side, and use the same side arm.

Scoop the leg from the knee back to the other leg; keep the other leg straight and body upright. Using the same motion for the arm, so just one side of the body is moving. Travel sideways in the direction of the scooping leg. Travel for as much distance as possible before Changing sides and using the other leg and arm to travel back the other way.

♥♥♥♥ More power and bigger scoops.

🔑 **Use the inner thigh to power back**

Your own notes:

_____

_____

_____

Long Thigh Squeezers

♥♥♥ Legs stretched out wide to each side. The body stays long and straight, with feet down towards the pool floor. Keeping abdominal muscles engaged, power straight legs inwards, keeping the feet flat until the thighs meet.

Keep the feet flat and power outwards as far as comfortable. Allow the arms to lower and raise as high and wide as comfortable to stabilise the body.

All the power is in the thigh muscles.

♥♥♥♥ Increase the power and speed.

⚷ **Squeeze the thighs**

Your own notes:

_____

_____

_____

Extended Heel Flicks

❤ ❤ Sitting in the water, back straight and both legs stretched forwards and close to the pool surface.

Bend one knee and try to bring the heel under the body while keeping the other leg as close to the surface and as straight as possible.

Return the leg to the start position and repeat with the other leg. Keep back as straight as possible and abs engaged and knees soft.

❤ ❤ ❤ Double pull arms to travel forward.

❤ ❤ ❤ ❤ Double forward scoop arms to travel backwards.

❤ ❤ ❤ ❤ ❤ Power sculling arms and very fast kicks to elevate shoulders out of the water.

🔑 **Power down**

Your own notes:

_____

_____

_____

Vertical Crunch

♥ ♥ ♥ Hanging long in the water with back straight and both legs stretched downwards and outwards. Power the inner thighs together, when they meet keep them long and straight. Pull the abdominal muscles in and up, bend the knees and lift the knees up to the chest.

Push legs downwards keeping them together and repeat.

Keep the knees soft on the downwards movement. Use arms to stabilise the body.

♥ ♥ ♥ ♥ Increase the power and speed.

🔑 **Abs tight**

Your own notes:

_____

_____

_____

Goal Kicks

♥ Long body, legs under hips, side to side sweep arms in opposition to the legs. Keep one leg straight and kick the other lower leg across the mid line, over the straight leg with the inside of the foot leading the kick, (as if you were passing a football). Bring the leg back to the start position and repeat with the other leg.

♥♥ Increase the power and speed.

🔑 Long legs

Your own notes:

_____

_____

_____

Deep Curl Twists

♥♥ Bring the knees up to the chest, twist to one side keeping the back upright, feet flat. Push the legs downwards until they are nearly straight. Bring the knees back to the chest and twist to the other side. The arms push in the opposite direction to the knees.

♥♥♥ Increase speed and power.

♥♥♥♥ Roll the knees over to the side further, until hip is close to the surface.,

🔑 **Twist from waist**

Your own notes:

_____

_____

_____

212

Sole Touches

♥ Long body Legs wide and feet towards the pool floor, keep back straight and abs engaged, pull both feet inwards, keeping knees wide until the soles of the feet are completely line up together.

Pull the joined feet as high as comfortable towards the buttocks.

Release the feet and return to start position. Use the arms to stabilise the body, legs wide, arms in, feet joined arms wide.

♥♥ Increase the power and speed but keep the knees soft

🔑 **Pull upwards**

Your own notes:

_____

_____

_____

Heel Touches

♥ Long body Legs wide and feet towards the pool floor, keep back straight and abs engaged, pull both feet inwards, keeping knees wide until the heels of the feet touch and the toes are turned outwards.

Pull the joined feet as high as comfortable towards the buttocks.

Release the feet and return to start position. Use the arms to stabilise the body, legs wide, arms in, heels joined arms wide.

♥♥ Increase the power and speed but keep the knees soft.

🔑 **Toes outwards**

Your own notes:

_____

_____

_____

Stomp

❤ With an upright body. Keep the feet just wider than hip width apart. Raise one knee out to the side as high as comfortable, keeping a flat foot and a soft knee, stomp it back down while raising the other knee. Repeat alternate legs. Push the opposite arm downwards as the knee raises. Try to build up speed.

❤❤ Increase the power and speed.

🔑 **Soft knees**

Your own notes:

_____

_____

_____

Horizontal Crunch

♥ ♥ Start by lying back so the body is flat on the surface of the water, long straight legs and toes just above the surface.

Engage the abdominal muscles, push the bottom down towards the pool floor, sit upright and reach towards the toes. (Keep the toes above the surface). Return back to the start position.

♥ ♥ ♥ Increase the power and speed.

🔑 Abs tight

Your own notes:

_____

_____

_____

Pedal Pushers

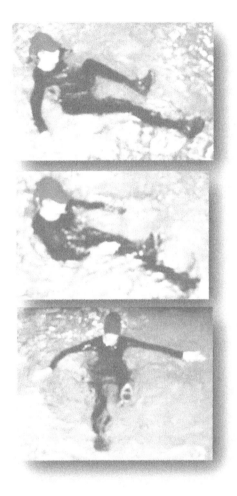

♥ ♥ Sit in a fairly upright position, and engage abs. Extend one leg keeping the sole of the foot half submerged. Bend the other knee towards the chest, again keeping half of the sole of the foot submerged. With soft knees push the legs alternately forcing the water forwards. (Pushing peddles).

Keep the same force on pulling the knee back as pushing the foot forward

Use any arm movement to keep the body in the same position.

♥ ♥ ♥ Increase the power and speed.

🔑 Feet ½ in ½ out

Your own notes:

_____

_____

_____

Elevating Cross Overs

♥♥♥ Shoulders, hips and ankles in line; abdominal muscles engaged throughout. Hands scull in line with the hips. Keeping the legs long and straight, cross on ankle over the other and repeat.

♥♥♥♥ On each cross over raise the legs a little higher until toes reach the surface.

♥♥♥♥♥ Keep feet above the surface of the water still crossing over.

♥♥♥♥♥♥ Keeping the abdominals engaged lower the legs on each cross over until they are under the hip.

Keep as a sequence or use in sections.

🔑 **Long straight legs**

Your own notes:

_____

_____

_____

Over and Outs

♥♥ Start with a long straight body. Both feet pointing towards pool floor. Cross one leg over the other, aiming for the foot to rest just above the knee joint, keep a wide knee, using the same leg power out to the side. Repeat for required reps and then change sides.

♥♥♥ Increase the power and speed but keep the knees soft.

🔑 **Lead with a flat foot**

Your own notes:

_____

_____

_____

Tuck Extension

❤❤ Start in a sitting position, knees tucked up to chest. Engage the abdominal muscles; push the feet upwards and outwards to the water surface, then pull downwards and inwards back to start position. Use arms to balance the body.

❤❤❤ Increase the power and speed.

🔑 **Abs tight**

Your own notes:

_____

_____

_____

Deep Stretches

Stretching in the deep can be challenging as the feet cannot touch the floor to stabilise the body. In traditional stretches the focus is on one limb at a time.

In the deep, keeping the centre of gravity and the centre of buoyancy aligned is the challenge, while stretching the worked muscles.

Keeping the aqua belt on will go some way to stabilising the body, but the other limbs need to be used to increase the stability while the muscles are being stretched. In addition, the need to keep the body warm must be taken into account.

Stabilisation is the key before attempting any stretch, otherwise the body will roll and the stretch will not be effective.

Deep Abductor Stretch

How: Balance in the water with a sitting position, use the arms to scull to help stabilise the body. Take legs as wide apart as possible and hold this position. Keep the arms moving to help with body balance.

Where: This stretch should be felt in the inner upper thigh.

How long: Hold 20/30 seconds.

Stay warm: Scull arms to keep head above the surface.

🔑 **Wide as possible**

Your own notes:

_____

_____

_____

Adductor Stretch

How: Sitting in the water, stretch legs out in front of you, toes pointed upwards. Cross one leg over the other at thigh height and avoid crossing on the knee joint. Try to separate the feet, while keeping legs long and straight. Swap over legs.

Where: This stretch should be felt in outer upper thigh.

How long: Hold 20/30 seconds and change over legs.

Stay warm: Sculling arms to keep above the surface.

🔑 **Separate feet**

Your own notes:

_____

_____

_____

Deep Quad Stretch

How: Balance the body by bringing one leg forward and use sculling arms. Keep the knee of the other leg pointing to the pool floor. Pull it back slightly and raise the heel upwards to the buttocks.

Where: This stretch should be felt in the front of the upper thigh of the backwards bent leg.

How long: Hold 20/30 seconds and change over legs.

Stay warm: Sculling arms.

🔑 **Hips forward**

Your own notes:

_____

_____

_____

Hamstring Stretch

How: Sitting in the water, stretch legs out in front of you, toes pointed upwards. Keep legs stretched, curl toes towards knees and either reach down to hold toes, or swing arms behind for easier balance.

Where: This stretch should be felt in the back of the upper thigh.

How long: Hold 20/30 seconds.

Stay warm: Sculling arms to keep above the surface.

🔑 **Curl toes upwards**

Your own notes:

_____

_____

_____

Deep Gastrocnemius Stretch

How: Balance the body by raising one knee forwards and arms wide. Stretch out the other leg behind the body, keeping the back straight. Curl toes up to knees and try to get the heel lower than the toes. Keep foot straight.

Where: This stretch should be felt in muscle of the back of the lower leg.

How long: Hold 20/30 seconds and change over legs.

Stay warm: Move arms backwards and forwards wide.

🔑 **Heel downwards**

Your own notes:

_____

_____

_____

Deep Pectoral Stretch

How: Wide legs to balance the body, bring both arms behind the body, bend the elbows and try to squeeze them closer.

Where: This stretch should be felt across the chest.

How long: Hold 20/30 seconds.

Stay warm: Move legs backwards and forwards.

🔑 **Squeeze shoulder blades together**

Your own notes:

_____

_____

_____

Deep Biceps Stretch

How: Bring both hands behind the body. Link the fingers together palms facing outwards and extend arms backward.

Where: This stretch should be felt in front of the upper arms.

How long: Hold 20/30 seconds.

Stay warm: Thigh squeezer legs.

🔑 **Extend arms**

Your own notes:

_____

_____

_____

Triceps Stretch

How: Keep legs moving in a wide treading water action to balance the body. Bring one arm over the chest and hold with the opposite hand.

Where: This stretch should be felt in the back of the upper arm.

How long: Hold 20/30 seconds and change arms.

Stay warm: Wide treading water legs.

🔑 **Pull arm inwards**

Your own notes:

_____

_____

_____

Abdominal Stretch

How: Lay flat on your back, bend your knees and tuck your feet under the body. Lower arms so fingers are facing the pool floor, raise the chest and extend the trunk.

Where: This stretch should be felt down the front of the body from the lower chest to pelvis.

How long: Hold 20/30 seconds.

Stay warm: Move arms towards feet and back again slowly.

🔑 **Long body**

Your own notes:

_____

_____

_____

Hip Stretch

How: Stretch one leg out in front of the body. Bend the other leg at the knee out wide and to the side and rest the calf on the upper thigh of the extended leg. Avoid placing the leg on the knee joint! Gently lower the bent knee down towards the pool floor.

Where: This stretch should be felt in hip area of the bent leg.

How long: Hold 20/30 seconds and change over legs.

Stay warm: Sculling arms to keep above the surface.

🔑 **Lower the knee**

Your own notes:

_____

_____

_____

Latissimus Dorsi Stretch

How: Long body supine in the water, raise arms above head keeping them in the water at all times. Try to grow taller by pulling upwards from the hip area and stretching the arms as far as possible.

Where: This stretch should be felt in the back.

How long: Hold 20/30 seconds.

Stay warm: Small thigh squeezers.

🔑 **Grow taller**

Your own notes:

_____

_____

_____

Trapezius Stretch

How: Keep legs moving, curl up and wrap the arms around the front of the body in a hug. Gently pull shoulders forwards and dip the chin down to the chest.

Where: This stretch should be felt in outer upper back.

How long: Hold 20/30 seconds.

Stay warm: Gently flutter kick or jog.

Squeeze

Your own notes:

_____

_____

_____

Aqua Equipment

Some aqua classes use additional aqua equipment like noodles, handbuoys, mitts, discs, floats and buoyant ankle cuffs. Many of these are pieces of equipment that are larger and more buoyant than a limb, so create a much greater surface area.

The noodle is a long sausage shaped foam type piece of equipment found in most pools and commonly  used in swimming lessons. The newer and less chewed the noodle is, the more buoyant it will be. The more marked the noodle is, the more likely it is to break when used for water exercises, and as the noodle gets older it becomes waterlogged and loses its buoyancy, which renders it useless for water exercise.

A noodle is ideal for a weak or unconfident person in shallow water if used for support, but not if used to increase the buoyancy. This could destabilise the body and end up with the participant under the water.

If they were not confident in the water at the beginning, they would have even less confidence after an incident like that and even in shallow water they might panic and you would need assistance to recover them.

Noodles can be held behind the body, in front of the body, in one hand or in both hands, wrapped around the back or front of the body, used under the arms or sat on or stood on.

Remember to release the hand grip periodically and keep the poolside clear when you have finished with them.

Handbuoys are hand held pieces of equipment, with a bar in the middle and two round buoyant ends.  The good ones have foam covering over the hand held grip to make them more comfortable to use and moulded end caps, so the ends do not fall off when used in forwards and backwards upright exercises.

The handbuoys are not weights. Weights in the water would cancel out the buoyancy, and handbuoys are designed to increase the buoyancy on downwards movements. Handbuoys are good for increasing the resistance and but they must be kept either on the surface of the water or underneath the water.

Handbuoys can be used pushing and pulling in front of the body, pushing and pulling to the side of the body, pushing downwards and controlling the upwards movement and behind the body. They can also be use held close to the body as stabilisers, especially good for isolated leg movements in deep water and for increasing the drag when travelling if held slightly wider than the body in a fixed position.

Remember to release the grip periodically and keep the poolside clear when you have finished with them..

Warning Bringing the handbuoys in and out of the surface of the water creates jarring of the shoulder joint.

Handbuoys should be avoided for anyone with shoulder, elbow, wrist and finger problems, and arthritis sufferers, also for pregnant women.

Ankle cuffs are buoyant cuffs strapped around the ankle, either by a clip or by Velcro. Some have straps under the feet to stop them riding up the legs, others do not.

Ankle cuffs can only be used by very competent swimmers with a good level of fitness. These buoyant cuffs challenge core control and destabilise the body, they increase the buoyancy by being thicker than the ankle and therefor push the body upwards.

If the body position is not correct the legs will flip to the surface either behind or in front depending on which way the body is tilting. This can cause serious problems i.e. drowning. If using the buoyant cuffs the recovery position from both supine and prone must be taught at the beginning of each session. If the participant cannot easily regain standing then the **must not** use the cuffs. The cuffs are usually used in conjunction with the handbuoys to give more stability to the body. They can be used in deep water or shallow water. The feet and the cuffs must remain under the surface of the water at all times. If the cuffs come up and out of the water it is very difficult to pull or push them back down, this could cause muscle injury as the body will be forced out of alignment.

Ankle cuffs are bulky items and must be in kept in their pairs (right and left leg). Keep the poolside clear when you have finished with and get the participants to pair them back up and link them together when they take them off.

Discs can be either foam or hard plastic, again usually hand held,

these are designed for exercise with finger or hand holds built in. These round pieces of equipment again increase the resistance when pushed and pulled upright through the water. When pushed down flat into the water they increase the buoyancy. Both types of disc float quite well, so it is easy to retrieve them when dropped in the water. The plastic discs are quite heavy out of the water so should be stored at low level or in a wheeled basket.

Keep the poolside clear when you have finished using them

Floats are blocks of foam type material usually used by swimmers. These are again hand held, although not actually designed for water exercises and holding them can compromise the finger and wrist joint if held too tightly or for too long. The float also increases the resistance if held upright against the water and increases buoyancy if pushed down flat through the water. Usually only used for a small portion of the session. Floats stack easily.

The floats are predominantly used for resistance work can be held in various ways.

Lightly hold the float with straight wrists close to the front of the body. Adjust the float height to ensure elbows and wrists are in line and straight. The float is then pushed and pulled forward and backwards, creating turbulence and increasing resistance for the arm muscles. Ideal for forward kicks, backward kicks, skis, rocking horse exercises.

Held in the forward position is ideal for any leg isolation exercises with use travel, upright cycling, jogging, legs only skis as holding the float will create a greater resistance and prevent the arms form moving. If using for travelling make sure the elbows and the wrists are in a straight line.

Held like this, will put a strain on the wrist joints!

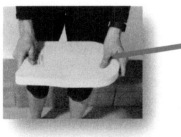

Held like this, will put a serious strain on the thumb joints!

Hugging the float will prevent any pressure on the wrist or thumb joints but can only be used for leg isolation exercises where you want to concentrate on body positioning, as it is very difficult to lean forwards if you are trying to keep the float straight and upright. Can be used for travelling and suspended exercises

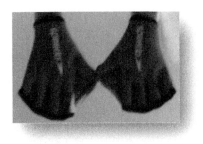 **Mitts** increase the surface area of the hand and can be used in three different ways, webbing – open hand, light fist and slicing – thumb up and little finger down. The material of the mitt will also increase drag as the water 'sticks' to the mitts. Some people with arthritis of the fingers find that soft mitts help with support. But that is an individual choice. You need to make the hand positions that you want very clear if teaching with mitts. Mitts are either Lycra (soft) or neoprene (hard), due to hygiene it is advisable that these are for personal use and owned and washed by the participant, if the mitts are not cleaned regularly they become slimy and smelly.

Equipment is usually used in the conditioning section of the class, or in the abdominal section. For a very fit class the handbuoys can be used in the aerobic section or throughout the whole session as well.

If you are using the equipment for a period of time, you need to give the participants additional exercises where they are not gripping the equipment.

For effectiveness, it depends on how the equipment is used and the equipment's position in the water as to how much resistance is added to the exercise, or how much buoyancy they add.

If the equipment is used in the wrong way, it can make the exercises much easier (or unsafe). Instead of using the core muscles for support, the participant relies on the noodle or handbuoys to give this support. This is not helpful to the core muscles.

Either way, care must be taken on who uses the equipment and how.

Try not to waste time and allow the participants to get cold by using the equipment for one or two exercises, putting it down, and then picking it up again a few minutes later. If you are going to use equipment, do all the exercises you need to do with it, then put it down and forget it.

Equipment Safety Please make sure when discarding equipment that it is put somewhere safe and not on the edge of the pool. If a pool evacuation is necessary, this will hinder clearing the pool area and also could be a trip hazard to your participants once they have exited the water.

Put them in a pile somewhere out of the way. You can collect them later and put them back in their basket. This is *your* job, not the lifeguard's job if you have one.

Also keep equipment clear of all emergency exits. You may need to use them and if the lighting fails although you will have emergency backup lighting, it's not very bright, and certainly not bright enough to try and clear an exit.

In our next section we will focus on the basic conditioning exercises and different positions and holds of the equipment.

Any downwards pushing to the pool floor will increase buoyancy, and any forwards, backwards and side to side pushing will increase the resistance. Both the noodles and the handbuoys can be used to challenge the balance of the core if used properly.

Stereos and sound equipment Battery operated sound equipment is the safest, especially rechargeable batteries, there are very few pools who will allow electrical equipment on pool side even wth a circuit breaker. All equipment must be kept away from the pool, place it somewhere safe so it does not get splashed by the water, far enough away so the participants can not touch it. If possible use a system that has a head mic inbuilt, all participants can hear you and it will save your voice. Pools are noisy places.

Noodle Exercises for Shallow Water

Jogging

♥ The noodle is held around the back of the upper body and the ends tucked under the arms. This gives the participant support and the ends of the noodle can be pushed down into the water.

The Noodle increases buoyancy when pushed down

♥♥ Jogging forwards and backwards.

♥♥♥ Increase speed and power.

🔑 **Stay upright**

Your own notes:

_____

_____

_____

Noodle Ski Legs

♥ The noodle is held around the back of the upper body and the ends tucked under the arms and hands resting on the ends of the noodle. Right leg extends forward as the left leg extends backwards. Tap the floor and change.

The Noodle aids balance

♥ ♥ Bounce the ski off the floor on the changeover of legs.

♥ ♥ ♥ Increase speed and power.

🔑 **Stay straight**

Your own notes:

_____

_____

_____

Noodle Ski

❤ ❤ The noodle is held around the back of the upper body and the ends tucked under the arms and hands resting on the ends of the noodle. Power one leg forward as the other goes backwards, arms in opposition. Right leg back,

left arm forward.

The Noodle increases resistance

❤ ❤ ❤ Bounce the ski off the floor on the changeover of legs.

❤ ❤ ❤ ❤ Increase speed and power.

❤ ❤ ❤ ❤ ❤ try to straighten the noodle.

❤ ❤ ❤ ❤ ❤ ❤ Keep feet off the floor and ski suspended, use the arms.

🔑 Long back leg

Your own notes:

_____

_____

_____

Rainbow Ski

♥ The noodle is held around the back of the upper body and the ends tucked under the arms and hands resting on the ends of the noodle. Right leg extends forward as the left leg extends backwards. Tap the floor and change.

The Noodle aids balance

♥♥ Bounce the ski off the floor on the changeover of legs.

♥♥♥ Increase speed and power.

🔑 **Stay straight**

Your own notes:

_____
_____
_____

243

Diagonal Ski

♥ Hold the noodle with one end in each hand about 9" from the very end of the noodle, sink the ends into the water. Right leg forwards as left leg goes backwards as left arm pushing the noodle goes forward and the right arm pushing the noodle goes backwards jump and swap arms/legs, keeping the noodle end in the water.

The Noodle increases resistance

♥♥ Bounce the ski off the floor when changing over the legs.

♥♥♥ Increase speed and power.

♥♥♥♥ Press down and back on the noodle adding extra resistance with ski arms, opposite arm to leg.

🔑 **Pull noodle round the side**

Your own notes:

_____

_____

_____

Ski Bars

♥ Holding the noodle in front of the body, aim to keep arms bent at elbow. Ski legs, one backwards one forwards, pushing the noodle forwards and pulling it backwards to your chest as the legs change over.

The Noodle increases the resistance

♥♥ Increase the speed.

♥♥♥♥ Take the feet off the floor (suspended) skis.

🔑 **Long legs**

Your own notes:

_____

_____

_____

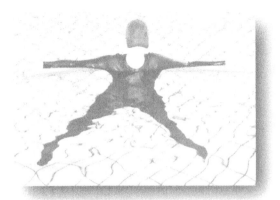

Noodle Jacks straight

♥ The noodle is held around the back of the upper body and the ends tucked under the arms and hands resting on the ends of the noodle. Both arms out to the sides, both legs out wide, bounce the legs and arms back together.

The Noodle *increases resistance*

♥♥ Bounce when the legs are out, bounce again when the legs come back together, same arms as above.

♥♥♥ Increase speed and power.

🔑 **Back straight**

Your own notes:

_____

_____

_____

Broomstick Challenge

♥ ♥ ♥ ♥ ♥ Start by sitting astride the noodle, make sure the noodle extends up your back, the front should just be long enough to balance your feet on with bent knees. Once sitting astride and balanced safely. Lean backwards and keep the arms wide to help stabile the body, place the feet on top of the noodle, one foot at a time. Using core muscles sit upright and push the feet and the noodle under the surface. Lean back slightly and repeat as often as possible.

Be aware of the noodle slipping and popping up through the water and hitting someone.

The Noodle increases buoyancy

🔑 **Abdominal muscles tight**

Your own notes:

_____

_____

_____

Noodle Jacks Hug

♥ ♥ The noodle should be held around the back of the upper body and the ends tucked under the arms and hands resting on the ends of the noodle. Both arms out to the sides, both legs out wide, bounce the legs and arms back together and cross over the arms at the front of the body, pushing the noodle.

The Noodle increases resistance

♥ ♥ ♥ Bounce when the legs are out, bounce again when the legs come back together, same arms as above.

♥ ♥ ♥ ♥ Increase speed and power.

🔑 **Back straight**

Your own notes:

_____

_____

_____

Jacks Noodle Behind

♥ Hold each end of the noodle, keeping it behind the back on the surface. Arms and legs extended out wide to each side. Jump the legs back together making sure the thighs meet. At the same time pull the noodle inwards so the ends of the noodle meet together under the surface of the water. Keep the elbows softly bent. Repeat

The Noodle increases resistance

♥ ♥ Increase the speed.

♥ ♥ ♥ Keep the inner upper arms on the noodle and squeeze.

♥ ♥ ♥ ♥ Hold the noodle higher up so more of the ends are under the water.

🔑 **Bounce in & squeeze**

Your own notes:

_____

_____

_____

Noodle High Kicks

♥ ♥ Noodle held behind the back, pushed low into the water. Keep back straight and abs connected kick up to the surface with one leg and then the other.

The Noodle increases buoyancy

♥ ♥ ♥ Bounce the kick and point the toes forward.

♥ ♥ ♥ ♥ Increase speed and power.

🔑 **Toes to surface**

Your own notes:

_____

_____

_____

Noodle Ankle Touches

♥Noodle held around the back of the upper body and the ends held in the hands lightly. Bending one knee outwards, pull the ankle upwards to meet the opposite side noodle end. Change legs and repeat.

The Noodle increases buoyancy and resistance

♥ ♥ Bounce and kick upward, bring the opposite noodle end forwards and backwards.

♥ ♥ ♥ Increase speed and power.

🔑 **Wide knees**

Your own notes:

_____

_____

_____

251

Rear Ankle Touches

♥ Then noodle is held around the back of the upper body and the ends held in the hands lightly, bring both hands back so they are at the side of the body. Bending one knee outwards push the heel of that foot across the back of the body and upwards to meet the opposite end of the noodle. Push the noodle backwards to meet the upcoming foot.

The Noodle increases resistance and buoyancy

♥♥ Increase the speed.

♥♥♥ Push the one end of the noodle forwards and the other end pushes backwards to meet the foot.

🔑 **Heel high**

Your own notes:

_____

_____

_____

Rocking Horse

❤Holding noodle in front of the body, hands just over hip width apart. Keep the noodle just under the surface of the water. Normal rocking horse, raise one leg with the noodle held close to the body, place the foot back on the floor and kick the other leg backwards, whilst pushing the noodle forwards.

The Noodle increases the resistance

❤❤ Increase the speed.

❤❤❤ Push the noodle further down under the water.

❤❤❤❤ Travel 4 forwards, 4 backwards.

🔑 **Push & pull**

Your own notes:

_____

_____

_____

Bow & Arrow

♥ Hold the noodle in the centre with one hand, lift the knee as high as comfortable on the same side as the hand that you are using. Lean forward and extend the arm with the noodle out front, using the same leg as the bent knee kick the leg out directly behind the body. Straighten up and bring the knee back to the front raised while adding a hop on the standing leg. Repeat then change sides.

♥ ♥ Increase the speed.

The Noodle increases the resistance

♥ ♥ ♥ Push the noodle further down under the water.

♥ ♥ ♥ ♥ Keep the standing foot static on the pool floor

🔑 **Push & kick**

Your own notes:

_____

_____

_____

Side Kicks Push Out

♥Hold the noodle behind the body, with a light grip on the end, lean the body to the right, stretching out the right arm and kick the left leg outwards. Pull the body over to repeat on the other side. Using a long arm to push and pull the noodle on the stretch out.

The Noodle increases resistance

♥♥ Increase the speed.

♥♥♥ Push the noodle further down under the water.

♥♥♥♥ Travel sideways in one direction and then travel the other way.

🔑 **Lean over**

Your own notes:

_____

_____

_____

Side Rocks Push Down

♥ Using one hand, hold the noodle in the centre. Push the noodle down under the water and with the opposite leg bent; raise the thighs and ankle to the surface. Pull upright and repeat a few times before changing sides.

The Noodle increases buoyancy

♥♥ Increase the speed.

♥♥♥ Push the noodle further down towards the pool floor then push out while it is still under the water.

♥♥♥♥ sideways in the direction of the hand with the noodle, change sides and travel the other direction.

 **Push down**

Your own notes:

_____

_____

_____

Twists

❤ Hold the noodle in front of the body about a $1/3^{rd}$ of the way from each end. Pull the noodle while under the water to one side and twist the body at the same time. Pull the noodle to the other side and twist again.

The Noodle increases resistance

❤❤ Increase the speed.

❤❤❤ Pull the noodle to the opposite side of the twist.

🔑 **Abs tight**

Your own notes:

_____

_____

_____

Balance Bar

♥ Hold the noodle in front of the body about a 1/3rd of the way from each end. Swing the noodle from left to right while the opposite leg rises upwards to the side with a flat foot and toes facing forwards. Pull the leg back sharply to centre.

The Noodle increases balance and resistance

♥♥ Increase the speed.

♥♥♥ Add a bounce and travel sideways.

🔑 **Toes forward**

Your own notes:

_____

_____

_____

Noodle side cycles

❤ ❤ Have the noodle stretched out in front or behind the body, long straight arms, roll onto the side, keeping hip on the surface, cycle around in a circle forward facing, using arms as drag, roll over and repeat.

The Noodle aids balance

❤ ❤ ❤ Increase the size of the leg movement.

❤ ❤ ❤ ❤ Push the lower arm down into the water at right angles to the shoulder, still holding the noodle.

🔑 **Stay on your side**

Your own notes:

_____

_____

_____

Pendulum

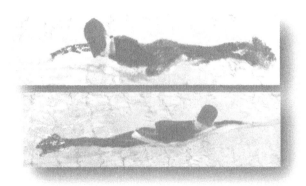

❤❤ Holding the noodle in the front of the body, about a 1/3rd of the way from each end. Keep the noodle close and stretch out on one side, keeping the upper shoulder clear of the water, curl knees up to a sitting position stabilise then stretch and push the legs out to the other side. Try to stay as straight as possible with hips on the surface and legs together.

The Noodle aids balance and increases resistance

❤❤❤ Increase the speed.

❤❤❤❤ Stretch to one side, pull to centre and stretch back to the same side. Repeat.

🔑 **Legs together**

Your own notes:

_____

_____

_____

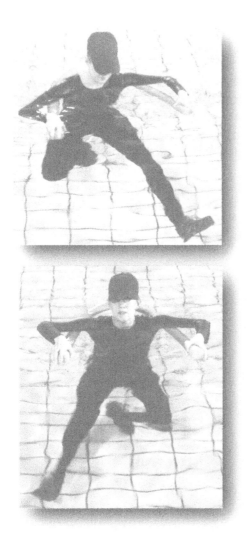

Floor Taps

❤❤ Hold the noodle close to each end, wrapped behind the body, rest elbows or upper arm on the noodle. With one leg kick out forward so heel taps the pool floor, with the other leg pull the foot inwards and backwards so the toe can tap the floor directly under the buttocks. Change legs and repeat.

The Noodle aids balance

❤❤❤ Increase the speed.

❤❤❤❤ Travel forwards.

🔑 **Back straight**

Your own notes:

_____

_____

_____

Side Jumps

❤❤ Hold the noodle in one hand placed in the centre. Push down into the water, keeping the shoulder down, back straight and abs tight. Jump the body to the opposite side, away from noodle and keeping the body straight. Push down on the noodle as you jump, keeping the arm long and balanced. Jump back to the centre and repeat. Change hands and repeat on the other side.

The Noodle increases resistance and aids balance

❤❤❤ Increase the speed.

❤❤❤❤ Push the noodle further out.

🔑 **Abs tight**

Your own notes:

_____

_____

_____

Noodle jumps

♥♥♥ Stand in the centre of the noodle with feet hip width apart. Hold your balance, engage the core muscles, bend your knees and bounce up and down.

The Noodle increases the buoyancy and challenges balance

♥♥♥♥ Increase the speed.

♥♥♥♥♥ Bring the knees higher up towards the chest, keeping body straight.

🔑 **Stand straight**

Your own notes:

_____

_____

_____

Noodle Heel Digs

♥♥ The noodle is held around the back of the body and then held in the hands lightly. The hands should be approximately hip width apart. Push both hands back so they are behind the body. Sink down into the water keeping core tight, kick one leg forward, tap heel on floor, other heel curls back towards the buttocks. Repeat with the other leg. Push and pull the noodle behind the body as each leg changes.

The Noodle increases buoyancy and resistance

♥♥♥ Increase the speed.

🔑 **Back straight**

Your own notes:

_____

_____

_____

Cheer Leader

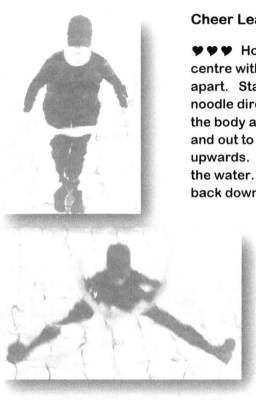

❤❤❤ Hold the noodle in the centre with both hands hip width apart. Standing straight, push the noodle directly downwards close to the body and lift both legs up wide and out to the side, toes pointed upwards. Try to get the toes out of the water. Power legs inwards and back down to a standing position and repeat. Keep back and legs straight.

The Noodle increases buoyancy

❤❤❤❤ Increase the speed.

🔑 **Power legs down**

Your own notes:

_____

_____

_____

Thigh Squeezers

♥ ♥ ♥ Sitting on the centre of the noodle, legs straight out in front, abs tight and toes pointed to the celling, aim to get your toes just above the surface. Pull the legs wide apart and then power them back together while remaining upright with a straight back.

The Noodle challenges balance

♥ ♥ ♥ ♥

Increase the speed.

♥ To make this easier wrap the noodle around the upper back and under the arms.

🔑 **Toes out**

Your own notes:

_____

_____

_____

Seated sole touches

♥ ♥ Sitting on the centre of the noodle, legs straight out in front, abs tight and toes pointed to the celling, Keeping back straight, pull one foot to aim to touch the inner thigh. Repeat with the other leg.

The Noodle challenges balance

♥ ♥ ♥ Increase the speed.

♥ ♥ ♥ ♥ To make this more challenging, as you pull one foot in, try to reach the opposite toe with your hand.

🔑 **Toes out**

Your own notes:

_____

_____

_____

Push Back Kicks

♥♥ Holding the noodle close to each end and behind the body, kick up with one leg, aim for the opposite arm and end of noodle to touch the toes, while pushing backwards with the other hand, (like ski arms) repeat with each leg or do a few reps on one leg and change over.

The Noodle increases resistance

♥♥♥ Increase the speed.

♥♥♥♥ Travel the exercise forward.

🔑 **Push back hard**

Your own notes:

_____

_____

_____

Right Angles

♥ ♥ Holding the noodle close to each end and behind the body with wide arms. Lean forward as much as possible. Swing one leg over the other to touch the end of the noodle in the opposite hand. Return to centre and repeat on the other side.

The Noodle aids balance

♥ ♥ ♥ Increase the speed.

🔑 **Stay straight**

Your own notes:

_____

_____

_____

Waist Whittler

♥ ♥ Holding the noodle close to each end and behind the body, Sit in the water and stay seated with back straight, bring heels up to your bottom and twist over to one side, come back to centre and repeat with the other side.

This can be done on one side only, always returning to centre.

The Noodle aids balance and control

♥ ♥ ♥ Increase the speed.

🔑 **Thighs to surface**

Your own notes:

_____

_____

_____

Noodle Running

♥ ♥ Holding the noodle in front of the body about hip width apart, take giant running steps travelling forward swishing the noodle from side to side.

The **Noodle increases resistance**

♥ ♥ ♥ Increase the speed.

♥ To make this easier bend the noodle and hold in front of the body and take smaller steps.

🔑 **Back straight**

Your own notes:

_____

_____

_____

Seated Cycle

♥♥ Sitting on the centre of the noodle with a straight back. Keep arms behind the body to use as extra drag. Extend legs forward and cycle. Keep toes in front of body.

♥♥♥ Increase the speed.

The Noodle challenges balance

♥ To make this easier wrap the noodle around the upper back and rest your hands on the ends, extend legs forward and cycle, keeping toes in front of the body.

The Noodle supports balance

🔑 **Use your heels**

Your own notes:

_____

_____

_____

272

Kickbacks

♥♥ Holding the noodle about 1/3rd from each end and keep it bent in front of the body. Push the noodle out and kick back with a long leg and flexed foot. Push down on the noodle as the leg comes back to start. Either repeat with the other leg, or do a few reps with one leg and then change legs.

♥♥♥ Increase the speed.

The Noodle increases resistance

🔑 **Lean forward back straight**

Your own notes:

_____

_____

_____

Single Hop Kicks

♥♥ Hold the centre of the noodle in one hand and push down to hip height. Hop on the leg the same side as the noodle. Quickly place the foot back on the floor and kick out with the other leg, leaning on the noodle and pushing it out to the side.

Repeat a few reps and change hands with the noodle and repeat exercise.

♥♥♥ Increase the speed.

♥♥♥♥ Add a bounce when replacing the foot.

The Noodle increases resistance and buoyancy

🔑 **Ankle bone to surface**

Your own notes:

_____

_____

_____

Side Curls

❤❤ With the noodle wrapped around the back of the body, place your hands on each end. Back straight and abs tight bring the heels up towards the buttocks, and roll the knees over to one side, aim to get the hips in line with the water surface. Roll the knees over to the other side and keeping the ankle bone pointing towards the surface straighten the legs. Do a few reps and then repeat on the other side.

❤❤❤ Increase the range.

*The **Noodle aids balance***

🔑 **Lean forward back straight**

Your own notes:

_____

_____

_____

Tuck Jacks

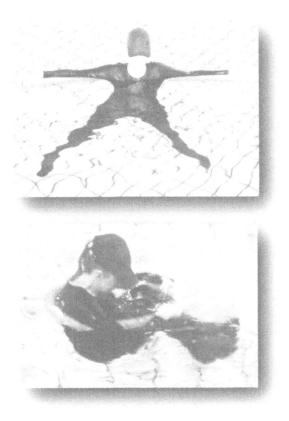

❤❤ Place hands on each end of the noodle, with the rest of the noodle behind the upper body and a straight line. Jump legs out to each side as wide as possible, then pull legs back in together and rise knees to chest height, bring arms forward to hug the knees, keeping the back straight. Push arms and legs back into the start position and repeat.

❤❤❤ Increase the speed and power.

The Noodle increases resistance

🔑 **Knees to chest**

Your own notes:

_____

_____

_____

Tuck Push

❤❤❤ The noodle is behind the body across the back of the shoulders. The arms are resting on the noodle and the hands holding each end.

Lie back in the water; keep the abdominal muscles engaged, and the heels just under the surface. Push the bottom towards the pool floor, sitting up slightly, bring the knees towards the chest, with the heels just under the surface. Bring the arms around and touch the noodle under the knees. Keep heels under and push legs straight out to start position, trying to move the water in front of the feet. Keep the knee joints soft

❤❤❤❤ Increase the speed and power but keep knees soft.

The Noodle increases resistance

🔑 **Noodle ends meet**

Your own notes:

_____

_____

_____

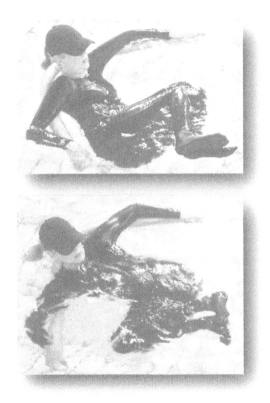

Turnovers

♥♥♥ The noodle is behind the body across the back of the shoulders. The arms are resting on the noodle and the hands holding each end. Lay back in the water, keep the abdominal muscles engaged. Keeping the legs firmly together, curl knees upwards, bringing the feet as close as possible to the buttocks. Back straight, arms relaxed, turn the legs over as far as comfortable, try to get the top leg thighs under the surface, then turnover to the other side. Try to keep the back straight and work from the waist.

♥♥♥♥ Increase the turn.

The Noodle aids balance

🔑 Hips up

Your own notes:

_____

_____

_____

278

Handbuoy Exercises for Shallow Water

Jogging with Handbuoys

♥ Hold the handbuoys in the centre bar so the handbuoy end caps are flat on the surface of the water. Use a light grip only, do not squeeze them. Normal jogging exercise, push the left arm forward as the right knee rises, and the right arm backwards, then change position.

♥♥ To increase the resistance greater turn the handbuoys up so the end caps face upwards and downwards and submerge in the water

The Handbuoys increase resistance

♥♥♥ Increase the speed.

♥♥♥♥ Push the handbuoys under the water.

🔑 Light grip

Your own notes:

_____

_____

_____

Ski with Handbuoys

♥ Holding the handbuoys in the centre, with the end caps facing upwards. Use a light grip, do not squeeze them. Normal Ski exercise, push the left arm forward as the right leg extends forwards and the right arm backwards as the left leg extends backwards, then swap position of the arms and legs. Keep the handbuoys under the water.

The Handbuoys increase resistance

♥♥ Increase the speed.

♥♥♥ Suspend the exercise.

Handbuoys increase buoyancy and resistance

🔑 **Long arms**

Your own notes:

_____

_____

_____

Ankle Touches with Handbuoys

♥ Holding the handbuoys in the centre with the end caps of the handbuoy facing upwards. Use a light grip, do not squeeze them. Raise the left ankle upwards and slightly towards the mid line, use the handbuoy to reach across the body pushing it down through the water and across slightly. Then change sides. Keep the handbuoys under the water.

The Handbuoys increase resistance and buoyancy

♥ ♥ Increase the speed.

♥ ♥ ♥ Hold the handbuoy out to the side of the body and power the sweep across for greater resistance.

🔑 Ankles to handbuoys

Your own notes:

_____

_____

_____

281

Wide Swing Ankle Taps

♥ Holding the handbuoys in the centre with the end caps of the handbuoy facing upwards. Use a light grip, do not squeeze them.
Raise the left ankle upwards and swing the leg across to the opposite side. Use the handbuoy to push forwards and if necessary downwards through the water to reach the foot. Swing the leg back to the standing position. Change sides. Keep the handbuoys under the water.

The Handbuoys increase resistance and buoyancy

♥♥ Increase the speed.

🔑 Ankles to handbuoys

Your own notes:

_____

_____

_____

Star Jumps with Handbuoys at Sides

♥ Hold the handbuoys in the centre with the ends of the handbuoy facing forwards and backwards just under the surface of the water. Arms and legs stretched out wide. With a light grip power the arms back to the side of the body and close the legs together. Keep the handbuoys under the water.

The Handbuoys increase buoyancy and resistance

♥♥ Increase the speed.

♥♥♥ Suspend the Exercise.

🔑 **Pull down control up**

Your own notes:

_____

_____

_____

Star Jumps with Handbuoys in the Middle

♥ Hold the handbuoys in the centre with the ends of the handbuoy facing forwards and backwards just under the surface of the water. Arms and legs stretched out wide. With a light grip power the arms back and legs back in, but this time the handbuoys meet in the middle of the body turned upwards. On the out power do not let the handbuoys come out of the water.

The handbuoys increase the resistance

♥♥ Increase the speed.

♥♥♥ Suspend the Exercise and have a knee tuck so the handbuoys are in front of the lower legs. *The handbuoys will increase resistance and buoyancy.*

🔑 **Pull down control up**

Your own notes:

_____

_____

_____

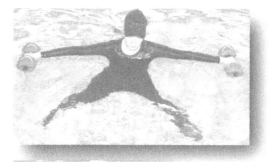

Star Jumps with Handbuoys at the Waist

♥ Hold the handbuoys in the centre with the ends of the handbuoys facing forwards and backwards just under the surface of the water. Arms and legs stretched out wide. With a light grip power the arms back and legs back in. The handbuoys get tucked into the waist with the elbows high. On the out power do not let the handbuoys come out of the water.

The Handbuoys increase resistance

♥♥ Increase the speed.

♥♥♥ Suspend the Exercise and change the format when the legs are out the handbuoys are at the waist, when the legs are in the handbuoys are out to the side.

⚭ **Elbows high**

Your own notes:

_____

_____

_____

285

Low Forward Kicks with Surface Handbuoys

♥ Hold the handbuoys on the centre bar, with the ends of the handbuoy facing outwards on the surface of the water. As the right leg kicks forwards the left arm pushes the handbuoy on the surface towards the kick and the right arm pulls the handbuoy backwards. Repeat with the other leg and arm.

The Handbuoys increase resistance

♥♥ Increase the speed.

♥♥♥ Keeping back straight use the handbuoys under the water.

🔑 **Back straight**

Your own notes:

_____

_____

_____

Low Forward Kicks with Upright Handbuoys

♥ Hold the handbuoys in the centre with the ends of the handbuoy facing upwards and downwards half submerged in the water. As the right leg kicks forwards the left arm pushes the handbuoy on the surface towards the kick and the right arm pulls the handbuoy backwards. Repeat with the other leg and arm.

The Handbuoys increase resistance

♥♥ Increase the speed

♥♥♥ Keeping back straight, lower the body until the shoulders are under the water and keep the handbuoys submerged.

🔑 **Pull back hard**

Your own notes:

_____

_____

_____

287

High Kicks with Handbuoys

♥ Hold the handbuoy on the centre bar with the ends of the handbuoy facing outwards. As the right leg kicks forward skim the handbuoy forward to touch the toes. Keep the other leg bent and submerge the handbuoy and pull back in a straight line past the hips. Change arms and legs and repeat.

The Handbuoys increase resistance

♥♥ Increase the speed.

♥♥♥ Keeping back straight, lower the body until the shoulders are under the water and keep both the handbuoys submerged.

🔑 **Push and pull**

Your own notes:

_____

_____

_____

Scissor Legs with Handbuoys

♥ Hold the handbuoys in the centre but this time with the ends of the handbuoy facing upwards keep in front of the body at mid height. Extend one leg forward and the other backwards. Change position of legs and move the handbuoys round the sides of the body until they meet at the lower back, change leg positions again and bring the handbuoys back round the sides of the body to the front. Repeat.

The Handbuoys increase resistance

♥ ♥ Increase the speed.

♥ ♥ ♥ Suspend the exercise.

🔑 **Balance the handbuoys**

Your own notes:

_____

_____

_____

Alternate Back Kicks with Handbuoys

♥ Hold the handbuoys in the centre with the ends facing outwards just under the surface of the water. Push the handbuoys forwards as one leg kicks straight back (keep a soft knee) add a jump as the leg comes back and the other leg kicks out.

Use the handbuoys for upper body work as the 2nd leg kicks out slightly turn the handbuoys upright and pull them to the centre until they touch, then push them forwards and wide again for the first leg kick out.

The Handbuoys increase resistance

♥♥ Increase the speed.

♥♥♥ Keep the shoulders under the water.

🔑 **Push out flat, pull in upright**

Your own notes:

_____

_____

_____

Alternate Back Kicks with Upright Handbuoys

♥ Hold the handbuoys in the centre with the ends facing upwards just under the surface of the water. Push the handbuoys forwards as one leg kicks straight back (keep a soft knee) add a jump as the leg comes back and the other leg kicks out.

The Handbuoys increase resistance

♥♥ Increase the speed.

♥♥♥ Keep the shoulders under the water.

🔑 **Push and pull**

Your own notes:

_____

_____

_____

Rocks with Handbuoys

♥ Submerge the handbuoys under the water, with the ends facing forward and back. Press down on the handbuoy and lift the opposite leg with a bent knee slightly outwards, rock back onto the other leg and repeat.

The Handbuoys increase buoyancy

♥♥ Increase the speed.

♥♥♥ Keep the shoulders under the water.

🔑 **Push down**

Your own notes:

_____

_____

_____

Power Rocks with Handbuoys

♥ Hold the handbuoys in the centre with the ends facing forwards and backwards. Keep the handbuoys just under the surface of the water. Extend one arm and power the handbuoy out to the side, keeping the handbuoy under the water, while leaning over in that direction. Lift the opposite leg upwards.

The Handbuoys increase resistance

♥♥ Increase the speed.

♥♥♥ Keep the shoulders under the water and pull the handbuoy into the waist.

🔑 Lean over

Your own notes:

_____

_____

_____

Power Kicks with Handbuoys

♥ Holding the handbuoys in the centre with the end caps facing outwards and under the surface of the water. Power one arm out to the side, keeping the handbuoy submerged and powering through the water. Kick the opposite leg out high, aim for just under the surface. Pull the handbuoy back to the hips with effort and repeat with the other handbuoy/leg.

The Handbuoys increase resistance

♥♥ Increase the speed.

♥♥♥ Travel to the side and return.

🔑 **Push and pull hard**

Your own notes:

_____

_____

_____

Double Pull Backs with Handbuoys

This exercise can use jogging, flutter kicks or low forward kick legs.

The focus is on the arms, chest and shoulders.

♥ Hold the handbuoys by the side of the body, the ends facing the body and side. Keep the handbuoys as submerged as possible, power the handbuoys forwards and backwards as far as comfortable.

The Handbuoys increase resistance

♥♥ Increase the speed.

♥♥♥ Travel forwards and backwards keeping the handbuoys low.

🔑 **Push and pull**

Your own notes:

_____

_____

_____

Rocking Horse Handbuoys

♥ Holding the handbuoys flat or upright down by the hips, lift the left knee upwards, power the leg back down, push the handbuoys forwards under the water, kick the right leg straight backwards, rock the body back upright pulling the handbuoys back to the hips, repeat a few times then change legs.

The Handbuoys increase resistance

♥♥ Increase the speed.

♥♥♥ Keep the shoulders under.

♥♥♥♥ Travel 4 forwards, change legs and travel 4 backwards.

🔑 **Extend**

Your own notes:

_____

_____

_____

Side Raisers with Handbuoys

♥ Holding the handbuoys flat or upright slightly in front of the body, push both handbuoys to the right while raising a straight left leg to the surface, Pull the handbuoys across the body and push out to the other side as the legs returns to centre and the other leg extends. Try to keep the leg straight.

The Handbuoys increase resistance

♥♥ Increase the speed.

♥♥♥ Keep the shoulders under.

♥♥♥♥ Travel 4 forwards, change legs and travel 4 backwards.

🔑 **Power the handbuoys across**

Your own notes:

_____

_____

_____

Single Leg Kicks with Handbuoys

♥ Balance on one bent leg, keep the handbuoys just in front of the body, kick the other leg forwards using the handbuoys for balance and then kick the same leg straight back behind, keeping a soft knee. The handbuoys push powerfully forward; bring the same leg back to kick in the front without touching the floor with the kicking leg. Repeat a few and change legs.

The Handbuoys increase resistance

♥♥ Increase the speed.

♥♥♥ Keep the shoulders under the water.

🔑 **Push out**

Your own notes:

_____

_____

_____

Single Taps with Handbuoys

♥ Balance on one bent leg, keep the handbuoys just in front of the body pushing down into the water. Tap the pool floor behind with one leg and using the same leg tap the floor in front of the body. Keep the handbuoys still and the leg straight while tapping.

The Handbuoys aid balance

♥♥ Increase the speed.

⚲ **Touch the pool floor**

Your own notes:

_____

_____

_____

Windmills

♥ Start with a wide stance, feet wider than hips, holding the handbuoys in the centre of the bar with the end caps facing out to each side.

Hold arm just behind the body, handbuoy under the water, power the handbuoy round to the front of the body and across to the other side, pull back to starting position and when half way back start with the other arm. Legs remain static, turning comes from the waist.

The Handbuoys increase resistance

♥♥ Increase the speed.

🔑 Windmill arms

Your own notes:

_____

_____

_____

Double Rock

♥ ♥ Rocking forward, kick one leg straight out behind while pulling the handbuoys held centre with the end caps facing upwards forwards in front of the body, rock backwards while lowering the back leg, when it has nearly reached the pool floor kick the other leg in front of the body while pulling the handbuoys out wide keeping the elbow bent. Repeat for a few reps then change legs.

The Handbuoys increase resistance

♥ ♥ ♥ Increase the speed.

♥ ♥ ♥ ♥ Add a bigger bounce to make the exercise more cardio.

♥ ♥ ♥ ♥ ♥ Travel the exercise forwards.

🔑 **Straight legs**

Your own notes:

_____

_____

_____

Single Leg 180

♥♥♥ Lean forward and lick one leg straight out behind the body, while pushing the handbuoys forwards, end caps facing upwards and downwards. Power the leg back through the water and kick straight out in front while pulling the handbuoys in a wide circle so they turn in the water and meet behind the body. Keep the elbows very slightly bent throughout the circle pull. Kick the same leg back behind the body and repeat a few reps, then change kegs

The Handbuoys increase resistance

♥♥♥♥ Increase the speed and power.

♥♥♥♥♥ Travel the exercise forwards.

🔑 **Pull**

Your own notes:

_____

_____

_____

Tucks

♥ ♥ Arms out wide, handbuoys under the surface of the water, legs out wide and evenly balanced. Core muscles engaged and keeping the back straight, power the handbuoys down by the sides of the body and at the same time, power the legs together and the knees up to the chest, than back out to the start position before landing on the pool floor with arms and legs wide. Repeat.

The Handbuoys increase buoyancy

♥ ♥ ♥ Increase the speed.

♥ ♥ ♥ ♥ Add more force so the body elevates up and out of the water

♥ ♥ ♥ ♥ ♥ Travel the exercise forwards.

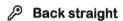 **Back straight**

Your own notes:

_____

_____

_____

Hop kick with Handbuoys

♥ Lift one knee up to the surface in a hop, at the same time the opposite arms pushes forwards. Power the foot back to the pool floor and kick the other leg upwards in a straight kick, the opposite arm reaches forward to touch the toes.   Repeat for a few reps before changing legs.

The Handbuoys increase resistance

♥♥ Increase the speed.

♥♥♥ Add bounce to make the exercise more cardio.

♥♥♥♥ Travel the exercise forwards.

🔑 **Soft standing leg**

Your own notes:

_____

_____

_____

Using Equipment In Deep Water

The equipment in deep has all the same benefits of using equipment in shallow water; the equipment used properly in the right position will increase the buoyancy and the resistance. Release the hand grips frequently to avoid strain on the finger and wrist.

The Noodle

Again the noodle can be used to increase buoyancy (downwards movements) and increase resistance with forward, backwards and sideways movement. Or use the equipment to combine both resistance and buoyancy challenges.

The noodle can be used in front of the body, held behind the body to cause extra drag, sat on to challenge the abdominal muscles, stood on (beware the noodle may pop up with some force so participants need to be aware they don't get hit by either their own noodle or someone else's).

The Handbuoys

As above they can be used to increase the downward force or the resistance, held by the side of the body to help with stability using opposing arm movements, or held static to challenge the core muscles.

The handbuoys must be either under the water, or on the surface, bobbing them in and out of the water will cause shoulder damage as the impact of the handbuoy breaking the surface will travel into the shoulder joint.

When using handbuoys the arms should never be fully extended to the sides, with the handbuoys on the surface, this is not an aligned body position and the body is hanging from the handbuoys and again putting excessive pressure on the shoulder joints, The buoyancy is elevating the body but still not enough for this type of movement. i.e. Jacks, keep the elbows slightly bent and hands lower than shoulders.

Elbow Cross Overs

♥♥ Hold each end and the rest of the noodle under the armpits and around the upper back of the body. Keeping the hand under the water, swish the noodle towards an out turned knee, aiming for the elbow to reach the knee and the noodle end and hands to stay under the water. Twist from the waist and extend the other leg out to the side while keeping it long and straight. Twist to the other side raising the long leg and straightening and extending the other.

The Noodle increases resistance

♥♥♥ Increase the speed.

♥♥♥♥ Travel forwards.

🔑 **Back straight**

Your own notes:

_____

_____

_____

Long Leg Cross Overs

❤❤ Noodle wrapped around the upper back. Hands resting on the ends, keep the back straight and tail bone pointed to the pool floor. Legs stretched forwards below the surface of the water. Cross one leg over the other with toes pointed forwards and abdominal muscles engaged.

The Noodle aids balance

❤❤❤ Increase the speed and cross the legs higher up.

❤❤❤❤ Use arm movements to travel forwards.

🔑 **Back straight, long legs**

Your own notes:

_____

_____

_____

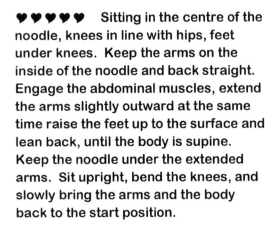

Deep T Crunch

♥♥♥♥♥ Sitting in the centre of the noodle, knees in line with hips, feet under knees. Keep the arms on the inside of the noodle and back straight. Engage the abdominal muscles, extend the arms slightly outward at the same time raise the feet up to the surface and lean back, until the body is supine. Keep the noodle under the extended arms. Sit upright, bend the knees, and slowly bring the arms and the body back to the start position.

♥♥♥♥ To make this exercise slightly easier keep the arms on the outside of the noodle with the hand holding as close to the ends as comfortable.

The Noodle increases the buoyancy

🔑 **Keep abdominals engaged**

Your own notes:

_____

_____

_____

Deep Ankle Touches

♥ ♥ Hold each end of the noodle and the rest of it under the armpits and around the upper back of the body. Keeping the hands under the water, push the end of the noodle downwards and inwards to meet the opposite leg, where the knee is turned out and the inner ankle bone is pulled upwards. Other leg sweeps slightly outwards but remains long, the other arm is static.

The Noodle increases resistance and buoyancy

♥ ♥ ♥ Increase the speed.

♥ ♥ ♥ ♥ Travel forwards.

♥ ♥ ♥ ♥ ♥ Twist from the waist as the noodle ends reaches down to the inner ankle.

🔑 Long legs

Your own notes:

_____

_____

_____

Deep Cossacks

♥ ♥ Hold each end of the noodle and the rest of it under the armpits and around the upper back of the body. Keep the hands just on the surface. Back straight and legs wide and downwards. Bring the sole of 1 foot up towards the opposite inner thigh and far as comfortable, return to the wide downwards position and repeat with the other leg. The arms are static resting on the noodle.

The Noodle aids stabilisation

♥ ♥ ♥ Increase the speed.

🔑 **Long legs**

Your own notes:

_____

_____

_____

Deep Reverse Travelling Cossacks

♥♥ The noodle is wrapped around the upper body under the armpits and held securely in front with the hands holding end of the noodle close to the body and crossed over. Keeping the back straight, the abdominals engaged and legs wide; slightly forward from the hips and low, bring the heel of one foot upwards and as close to the inner thigh as possible, kick the leg with the heel leading back to the start position using the heel to push the water forward. Keep the knees soft.

The Noodle aids stabilisation

♥♥♥ Increase the power of the legs.

🔑 **Power from the heels**

Your own notes:

_____

_____

_____

Deep Skis Noodle Behind

♥♥ The noodle is wrapped around the upper back under the armpits and held at each end lightly.

Use the arms and legs in opposition extend one arm forward, the other arm backwards, the opposite leg forwards and the other leg backwards. Use the noodle to create extra resistance as the arms and legs swap positions. Keep the back straight and the legs longs.

The Noodle increases resistance

♥♥♥ Travel forwards.

🔑 **Extend the rear leg**

Your own notes:

_____

_____

_____

Deep Skis Noodle Front

❤❤ The noodle is held in front of the body with a light grip

Use the arms and legs in opposition extend one arm forward, the other arm backwards, trying to straighten the noodle. At the same time the opposite leg forwards and the other leg backwards. Use the noodle to create extra resistance as the arms and legs swap positions. Keep the back straight and the legs longs.

The Noodle increases resistance

❤❤❤ Travel forwards

🔑 **Long arms close to the body**

Your own notes:

_____

_____

_____

Deep Vertical Lifts

♥ ♥ ♥ Long upright body, core engaged, stand in the centre of the noodle with hands held wide just under the surface area, scull with the hands. Without allowing the body to lean forward, lift the knees up to the chest, keeping the noodle stable and under the feet. Push the noodle back to starting position and repeat with control.

The Noodle increases buoyancy

♥ ♥ ♥ ♥ Travel forwards with breast stroke arms.

🔑 **Feet hip width apart.**

Your own notes:

_____

_____

_____

Deep Cheer Leaders

♥♥♥ Holding the noodle pushed below the thighs in front of the body. Hands hip width apart, legs together. Power both legs upwards and outwards with the toes pointing to the surface. Power back down again and return to start position. Keeping the back straight and the abdominals engaged.

The Noodle increases buoyancy

♥♥♥♥ Increase the speed and power

🗝 **Power legs down**

Your own notes:

_____

_____

_____

Noodle Hugs

❤ ❤ Noodle held around the back of the upper body and the ends tucked under the arms and hands resting on the ends of the noodle. Arms and legs stretched out to the sides. Power the legs back together and squeeze the thighs, at the same time pull the arms and the noodle around to the front, cross arms and hug the body.

The Noodle increases resistance

❤ ❤ ❤ Increase speed and power.

🔑 **Power in**

Your own notes:

_____

_____

_____

Noodle Squeeze

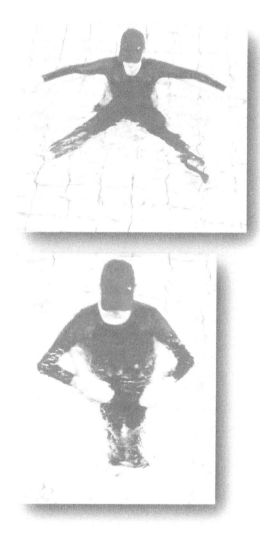

♥♥ Noodle held around the back of the upper body and the ends tucked under the arms and hands resting on the ends of the noodle. Arms and legs stretched out to the sides. Power the legs back together and squeeze the thighs, keep abdominal muscles engaged. At the same time pull the arms and the noodle around to the front. Keep the legs long and straight

The Noodle increases resistance

♥♥♥ Increase speed and power.

🔑 **Back & legs straight**

Your own notes:

_____

_____

_____

Noodle Bounce

♥♥♥ Using both feet stand in the centre if the noodle. Abdominal muscles engaged throughout. Keep the back straight. Lift the knees and lower in a bouncing movement. Make sure the noodle stays under the feet. Keep the knee joints soft.

The Noodle increases buoyancy

♥♥♥♥ Increase speed and height.

♥♥♥♥♥ Add breaststroke arms to travel forwards.

Be aware of the noodle slipping and popping up through the water and hitting someone.

🔑 **Back straight**

Your own notes:

_____

_____

_____

Noodle Sway

♥♥♥♥ Using both feet stand in the centre if the noodle. Abdominal muscles engaged throughout. Keep the back straight as possible and the tail bone pointing to the pool floor. Raise the knees to the chest.

Lower the legs slowly, keep the knees bent and push slightly forwards, maintain the balance, stay on the noodle. Bring the legs back under the body and return to crouched position.

The Noodle increases buoyancy

♥♥♥♥♥ Increase the distance of the forward push.

Be aware of the noodle slipping and popping up through the water and hitting someone

🔑 **Core engaged**

Your own notes:

_____

_____

_____

319

Seated Cross Overs

❤ ❤ Sitting on the centre of the noodle, core engaged arms outside of the noodle. One leg stretched downwards and slightly outwards, Bend the other leg at the knee, with the knee pointing outwards. Swing the foot over the straight leg aiming for above the knee, swap over with the other leg. Use the arms to maintain balance.

The Noodle challenges stabilisation

Be aware of the noodle slipping and popping up through the water and hitting someone

🔑 Long legs

Your own notes:

_____

_____

_____

Toe Touches

♥♥♥ With the noodle held around the back of the upper body and the ends tucked under the arms with the hands holding each end of the noodle.

Keeping the body long and vertically straight power one leg up towards the surface as high as is comfortable, aiming for the surface of the water. Use the opposite hand with the end of the noodle to reach the foot, power the leg back down and repeat with the other leg.

The Noodle increases resistance

♥♥♥♥ Increase speed and power

🔑 **Power down**

Your own notes:

_____

_____

_____

Toe Flick Touch

❤❤ With the noodle held around the back of the upper body and the ends tucked under the arms with the hands holding each end of the noodle. In a seated position with knees in line with hips, flick one leg upwards aiming for the toes to break the surface of the water and the other heel backwards to the buttocks. Keep knees level. Bring the opposite arm forward to reach the toes and the other arm backwards slightly just past the hips.

Keep the knees level and change legs and arms.

The Noodle increases resistance

❤❤❤ Increase speed and power.

🔑 **Knees together**

Your own notes:

_____

_____

_____

Unbalanced Heel Flicks

♥ ♥ ♥ Holding the noodle 1/3rd from each end, push under the water until it is under the buttocks but not touching the body. Keep the back straight, extend both legs forwards and toes just out of the water. Bring the heel of one leg back to touch the bottom of the noodle, return to the toes out position and repeat with the other leg.

The Noodle increases buoyancy and challenges stabilisation

♥ ♥ ♥ ♥ Increase speed and power.

🔑 **Kick back sharply**

Your own notes:

_____

_____

_____

Noodle side cycle

♥ ♥ ♥ Laying on one side, hold the noodle in the centre with one hand, use an open palm hold. Keeping the elbow slightly bent and the noodle position 90 degrees under the shoulder.

Cycle round in a forward facing circle, keeping the upper shoulder clear of the water. Use the legs to propel the body. After one circle change arms and repeat

The Noodle challenges balance and increases buoyancy

♥ ♥ ♥ ♥ Increase the size of the leg movement.

🔑 **Stay on your side**

Your own notes:

_____

_____

_____

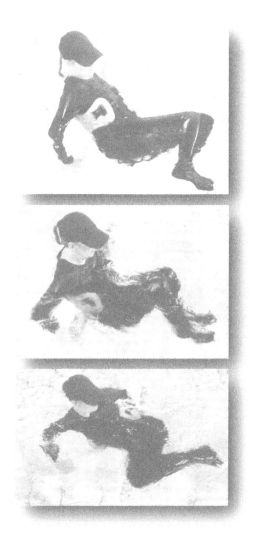

Challenge Twisters

♥ ♥ ♥ Hands on the noodle hip width apart, held behind the body in line with the tail bone but not touching the body. In a sitting position and keeping the knees together, bring the heels as close to the buttocks as comfortable.

Engage the core muscles, keeping the knees high, roll over from the waist and try to get the hip to the surface. Return to centre and repeat the other side.

The Noodle challenges balance and increases buoyancy

🗝 **Feet close to buttocks**

Your own notes:

_____

_____

_____

Pendulum Swings

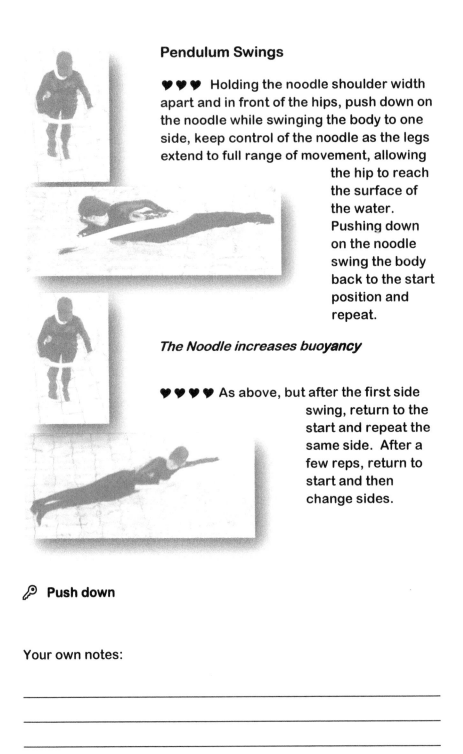

♥♥♥ Holding the noodle shoulder width apart and in front of the hips, push down on the noodle while swinging the body to one side, keep control of the noodle as the legs extend to full range of movement, allowing the hip to reach the surface of the water. Pushing down on the noodle swing the body back to the start position and repeat.

The Noodle increases buoyancy

♥♥♥♥ As above, but after the first side swing, return to the start and repeat the same side. After a few reps, return to start and then change sides.

🔑 **Push down**

Your own notes:

_____

_____

_____

Push Backs

❤❤❤ Holding the noodle just wider than shoulder width apart. Push down into the water with a loose grip. Push the legs out behind the body at an angle and keeping the body in a straight line, feet lower than knees, knees lower than hips, hips lower than shoulders. The elbows remain slightly bent.

Using the core muscles bring the knees upwards towards the noodle, and then push back to the start position. Try to keep the static.

The Noodle increases buoyancy

🔑 **Long legs**

Your own notes:

_____

_____

_____

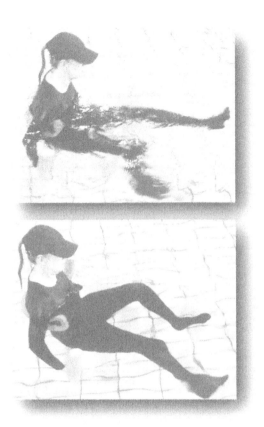

Cycle Challange

♥ ♥ ♥ Holding the noodle 1/3rd from each end, push under the water until it is under the buttocks but not touching the body.

Keep the back straight, and the abdominal muscles engaged, extend one leg forward, driving the heel down and round in a circle, keeping the feet softly flexed, then repeat with the other leg in a cycling motion. Try to keep the knees under the water and the feet in front of the hips.

The Noodle increases buoyancy

♥ ♥ ♥ ♥ Push the noodle slightly behind the body then increase the speed and power.

🔑 **Power heels down**

Your own notes:

_____

_____

_____

Balanced Crunch

♥♥♥ Sitting in the centre of the noodle, extend the legs forward but keep as low as possible. Keep the arms on the inside of the noodle and back straight. Engage the abdominal muscles, extend the arms slightly outwards at the same time bend the knees and pull upwards to the surface, keeping the feet in front of the knees. Allow the arms to come to the centre. Using the heels, push the feet back to the start position and widen the arms slightly.

The Noodle increases buoyancy

♥♥ To make this slightly easier have the arms on the outside of the noodle but not holding on.

🔑 **Keep balanced**

Your own notes:

_____

_____

_____

Reverse Flutters

♥♥♥ Holding the noodle behind the body, hands on the noodle just over hip width apart. Push the noodle away from the body ad far as comfortable making sure the back of the hands are facing towards the body. Angle the legs slightly forwards, keeping the abdominal muscles engaged, kick from the knees downward small and fast to travel in reverse.

The Noodle increases buoyancy and the resistance.

♥♥ To make this slightly easier have the noodle wrapped around the upper back of the body and under the armpits. The hands can rest on the noodle.

🔑 **Long body**

Your own notes:

_____

_____

_____

Y Sits

❤❤❤ With the noodle held around the back of the upper body and the ends tucked under the arms with the hands holding each end of the noodle. Lay back in the water, feet and hips on the surface, toes just out of the water. Arms spread wide above the shoulders. Push the bottom down in the water while bringing arms forward to hug bent knees, return to start position with core engaged at all times, Keep hands and noodle under the water.

The Noodle increases the resistance

❤❤ To make this slightly easier take arms to shoulder height.

🔑 **Push bottom down**

Your own notes:

_____

_____

_____

Y Crunches

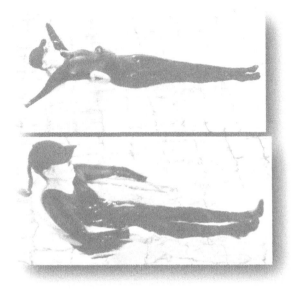

❤❤❤ The noodle is held around the back of the upper body and the ends tucked under the arms with the hands holding each end of the noodle. Abdominal muscles engaged at all time. Lay back in the water, feet and hips on the surface, toes just out of the water. Arms spread wide above the shoulders. Push the bottom down in the water while bringing arms forward. Keep the legs long and straight and toes out of the water. Return to start position and repeat.

The Noodle increases the resistance

❤❤ To make this slightly easier take arms to shoulder height.

🔑 **Push bottom down**

Your own notes:

_____

_____

_____

Noodle Jumps

♥♥♥ Holding the noodle shoulder width apart and in front of the hips, keep a long straight body with the core engaged throughout. Push down on the noodle lifting both knees high to jump over the noodle keeping the back straight.

Jump completely over the noodle and push the legs forwards and downwards keeping the noodle close behind the body but not sitting on it. Reverse the action by jumping backwards over the noodle and pushing the legs straight downwards.

The Noodle increases buoyancy

🔑 **Over & back**

Your own notes:

_____

_____

_____

Half Jumps

♥♥♥♥ Holding the noodle shoulder width apart and in front of the hips, keep a long straight body with the core engaged throughout. Push down on the noodle lifting both knees high to jump up until the feet are in line and just over with the noodle. Remain balance and keeping the arms as still as possible push both legs backwards and outwards, keeping the feet in line with the hips and the hips in line with the shoulders. Keep the back straight throughout. Avoid returning the feet to the floor, from the angled position bring the knees up and swing back to having the feet just above the noodle. Repeat.

The Noodle increases buoyancy

♥♥♥ To make these exercises easier, return feet to the floor and push off lightly to jump position.

Up and back

Your own notes:

_____

_____

_____

Side Crunches

♥ ♥ ♥ Holding the noodle in one hand directly under the shoulder, use an open hand hold. Bring the knees up to the chest, core muscles stay engaged throughout, hold the balance. Push the noodle towards the pool floor and push the feet over to the opposite side to the noodle and extend the legs downwards and slightly outwards. Keep the body in a straight line and the feet as close to the pool bottom as possible. Bend the knees and pull the body back to the balanced start position. Repeat and then change sides.

The Noodle increases the buoyancy

🔑 **Stay straight**

Your own notes:

_____

_____

_____

Shoot Through

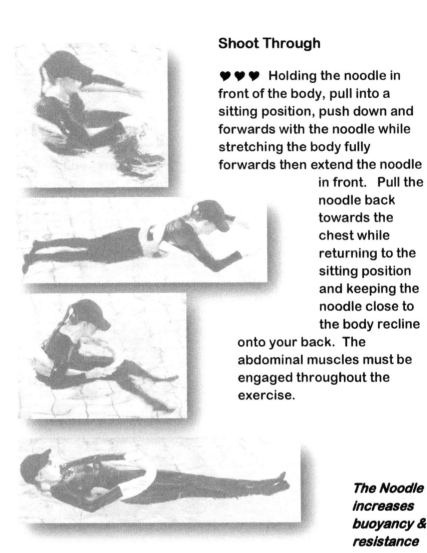

♥♥♥ Holding the noodle in front of the body, pull into a sitting position, push down and forwards with the noodle while stretching the body fully forwards then extend the noodle in front. Pull the noodle back towards the chest while returning to the sitting position and keeping the noodle close to the body recline onto your back. The abdominal muscles must be engaged throughout the exercise.

The Noodle increases buoyancy & resistance

🔑 **Sit & stretch**

Your own notes:

_____

_____

_____

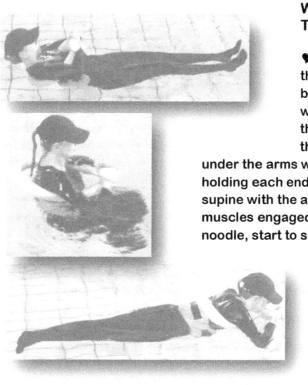

Wrapped Shoot Through

♥ ♥ ♥ Similar to the Shoot Through but the noodle is wrapped around the upper back of the body, held under the arms with a hand holding each end. The body start supine with the abdominal muscles engaged. Holding the noodle, start to sit up and at the same time bend the knees and pull the feet in until they are just under the knees. Extend the hands so the end of the noodle come forward by the face, roll forwards and stretch the legs out behind. Lower the legs and bring the knees up until the body has tilted upright in the sitting position then repeat.

The Noodle increases buoyancy & resistance

🔑 Sit , roll, stretch

Your own notes:

_____

_____

_____

Broomstick

♥♥♥ Sitting on the noodle like a broom stick, hold the end of the noodle between the ankles making sure the legs and feet are straight. Engage the core muscles and raise and lower the legs as far as comfortable. Keep the back straight throughout and use the arms to balance the body.

The Noodle increases buoyancy

♥♥♥♥ Make the movements bigger but keep control.

.Be aware of the noodle slipping and popping up through the water and hitting someone

🔑 **Slowly**

Your own notes:

_____

_____

_____

Push Outs Swing

♥ ♥ ♥   Holding the noodle slightly bigger than hip width apart and keep under the water just behind the body. Keep the elbows bent and a light grip. Lean back slightly not allowing the body to touch the noodle, tuck the knees up to the chest. Sitting upright and pulling the noodle forwards just under the hips while straightening the leg out in front. Again do not allow the noodle to touch the body. Push the noodle and the body back to the start position while bending the knees. Keep the core engaged throughout the exercise.

The Noodle increases buoyancy & resistance

🔑 **Abdominals engaged**

Your own notes:

_____

_____

_____

339

Thigh Squeezer Swing

♥♥♥ Holding the noodle slightly bigger than hip width apart and keep under the water just behind the body. Keep the elbows slightly bent and a light grip. Keeping the back straight and the core engaged, open the legs as wide as comfortable, and the feet just breaking the surface. Pull the noodle from behind the body to under the buttocks while powering the thighs back together. Push the noodle backwards as the legs open.

The Noodle increases buoyancy & resistance

🔑 **Power in**

Your own notes:

_____

_____

_____

Wide Cross Overs

♥♥♥ Wrap the noodle around the back of the upper body and tuck it under the armpits, holding onto the noodle sit in the water, back straight and abdominal muscles engaged. Sweep legs out to the sides as wide as comfortable and power in again and cross the legs. Aim to cross the legs above the knee, power out with control and repeat.

♥ To make this easier cross the legs at the ankles.

The Noodle increases buoyancy & resistance

🔑 **Power out, power in**

Your own notes:

_____

_____

_____

Handbuoy Exercises for Deep Water

Skis

♥ ♥ ♥ Light grip on the handbuoys with the ends either facing upwards or outwards, push the right arm forward and the right leg backwards, the left arm backwards and the left leg forwards. Keeping at least half the handbuoys submerged. Change position of arms and legs all at the same time. Try to make the arms and legs full range of movement. Abdominals engaged throughout and back straight.

♥ ♥ ♥ ♥ Increase the range and speed.

♥ ♥ ♥ ♥ ♥ Travel forwards

♥ ♥ ♥ ♥ ♥ ♥ Travel backwards

The Handbuoys increases buoyancy & resistance

🔑 **Long legs**

Your own notes:

_____

_____

_____

Jacks In Opposition

❤ ❤ Hold the handbuoys in the centre and with long arms stretched out to the sides and handbuoys submerged. Legs together and toes pointed forward. Engage the core muscles; pull the handbuoys downwards in front of the body while stretching the legs out wide. Control the handbuoys back to the wide arm start position (not allowing them above the surface of the water) and power the thighs back together.

❤ ❤ ❤ Increase the speed.

❤ ❤ ❤ ❤ Try to lift the shoulders out of the water as the arms power down and then again as the legs power together.

The Handbuoys increases buoyancy

🔑 **Stay straight**

Your own notes:

_____

_____

_____

343

Long Ankle Taps

❤ ❤ Hold the handbuoys in the centre ends facing forwards. Keep a long body, raise on knee out to the side and bringing the foot inwards, use the opposite arm to reach across and touch the ankle. The other arm stays wide under the water and the other leg stays long and extended outwards to balance the body, change legs and arms at the same time.

❤ ❤ ❤ Increase the speed.

*The **Handbuoys increases** buoyancy*

🔑 **Long wide legs**

Your own notes:

_____

_____

_____

Rear Ankle Taps

♥ ♥ Hold the handbuoys in the centre ends facing forwards. Keep a long body. Extend one straight leg forwards keeping the heel pointed to the pool floor and the other leg backwards bring the heel up towards the buttocks with a slight turned out knee. Reach the opposite arm around the body to touch the heel, then swap legs.

♥ ♥ ♥ Increase the speed and power of the arms.

The Handbuoys increases resistance & buoyancy

🔑 **Make contact**

Your own notes:

_____

_____

_____

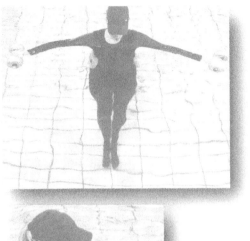

Knees Up

❤ ❤ Hold the handbuoys in the centre ends facing forwards. Keep a long body hanging in the water, arms outstretched with a slight bend of the elbows and handbuoys under the surface of the water. With power pull the handbuoys into the side of the body; maintain long arms with a slight bent elbow. At the same time bring the knees up to the surface of the water, keep the abdominal muscles engaged and the feet together just under the knees. Return to start position and repeat.

❤ ❤ ❤ Increase the speed.

The Handbuoys increases the resistance & buoyancy

🔑 Hands down, knees up

Your own notes:

_____

_____

_____

Knees Hug

❤❤❤ Hold the handbuoys in the centre ends facing forwards. Abdominal muscles engaged hold a long body hanging in the water, arms outstretched with a slight bend of the elbows and handbuoys under the surface of the water. With power pull the handbuoys round the body. At the same time bring the knees up to the surface of the water and the feet slightly forward. Hug the knees, keeping the handbuoys at least half submerged. Return to start position and repeat.

❤❤❤❤ Increase the speed.

The Handbuoys increases the resistance

🔑 **Back straight**

Your own notes:

_____

_____

_____

Thigh Touches

♥ ♥ Hold the handbuoys in the centre with the ends facing upwards. Hold handbuoys in front of the body with bent elbows, while kicking one leg forward and the other leg with a wide knee and the foot coming towards the inner thigh. Pull the handbuoys apart while changing legs. Repeat.

♥ ♥ ♥ Increase the speed.

The Handbuoys increases the resistance

🔑 Back straight

Your own notes:

_____

_____

_____

Balanced Ski Legs

❤❤ Hold the handbuoys in the centre with the ends facing backwards and forwards. Balance the body with long arms and long legs. Extend one leg forward and the other leg backwards as far as comfortable. Without moving the arms change legs and repeat.

❤❤❤ Increase the speed and range.

The Handbuoys increases the buoyancy

🔑 **Long legs**

Your own notes:

_____

_____

_____

Tuck Touch

♥ ♥ Hold the handbuoys in the centre with the ends facing upwards and downwards. Long arms either side of the boy. Knees level with hips, back straight and abdominal muscles engaged. Extend one leg forward, toes to the surface while keeping the other leg static, use the same side arm to reach forward and touch toes with the handbuoy. Pull back to the start position and repeat with the other leg.

♥ ♥ ♥ Increase the speed and range.

The Handbuoys increases the buoyancy

🔑 **Stay balanced**

Your own notes:

_____

_____

_____

Flutters

♥ ♥ Hold the handbuoys in the centre with the ends facing forwards and backwards. Have long arms close to either side of the body and keep them still.

Keep the legs long and straight with a soft ankle and make tiny kicks keeping the feet under the body.

♥ ♥ ♥ Increase the speed.

♥ ♥ ♥ ♥ Try to kick fast enough to raise the shoulders out of the water.

The Handbuoys increases the buoyancy

🔑 **Long legs**

Your own notes:

_____

_____

_____

Pull Ups

❤❤❤ Hold the handbuoys in the centre with the ends facing to the side. Push handbuoys down into the water with slightly bent elbows and keeping the handbuoys under the body, and shoulder width apart. Push both legs out behind the body with the feet pointing to the pool floor and keep the body straight. Sharply pull the body into a sitting position whilst pushing the handbuoys a little lower in the water. Push the body back to the start position and repeat.

❤❤❤❤ Increase the power.

The Handbuoys increases the buoyancy

🔑 **Back straight**

Your own notes:

_____

_____

_____

Shoot Through

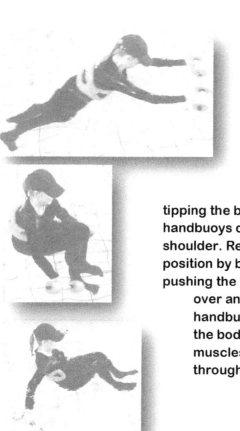

♥ ♥ ♥ Holding the handbuoys ends pointing to each side in front of the body, pull into a sitting position, push down and backwards with THE handbuoys while tipping the body backwards. Push the handbuoys downwards in line with the shoulder. Returning to the sitting position by bending the knees, pushing the handbuoys forwards, tip over and stretch out with the handbuoys stretched in front of the body. The abdominal muscles must be engaged throughout the exercise.

The Noodle increases buoyancy & resistance

🔑 **Stretch sit stretch**

Your own notes:

_____

_____

_____

Leg Swings

❤❤❤ Hold the handbuoys in the centre with the ends facing upwards and downwards. Lie on your side in the water with the arms extended and the handbuoys together. Try to keep the top hip on the surface and avoid rolling forwards or backwards. Stretch the legs out in line with the body, when balanced sweep the top leg as far forwards and backwards as is comfortable, maintaining control, keep the handbuoys as still as possible and keep the body balanced. Repeat for a few reps, roll over onto the other side and repeat with the other leg.

❤❤❤❤ Softly point the toes to increase leg length.

❤❤❤❤❤ Increase the power and the range.

The Handbuoys increases the buoyancy

🔑 **Stay balanced**

Your own notes:

_____

_____

_____

Crocodile Snaps

♥♥♥ Hold the handbuoys in the centre with the ends facing upwards and downwards. Lie on your side with the body angled feet lower than hips. Hips lower than shoulders. Use the handbuoys to balance the body so it does not roll forwards, stretch the legs out and without moving the lower leg raise the tip leg as high towards the surface as possible, then lower with force and control back to the bottom leg. Aim to keep the handbuoys still and keep control of the body. Repeat, change sides and repeat.

♥♥♥♥ Softly point the toes to increase leg length.

♥♥♥♥♥ Increase the power on lowering the upper leg.

The Handbuoys maintain balance

🔑 **Snap together**

Your own notes:

_____

_____

_____

Sole Touches

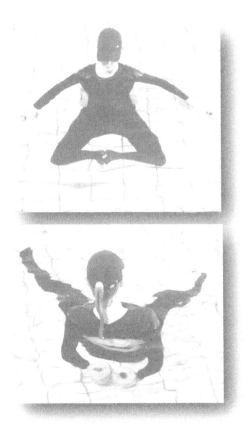

♥ ♥ ♥ Have an upright body, back straight, handbuoys held in each hand with the end facing forwards and backwards. Extend the arms downwards to balance the body, keeping the handbuoys under the water. Place the soles of the feet together, directly under the body. Push feet upwards and wide at the same time (try to reach the surface) pull the handbuoys behind the body, turning them as the move until the handbuoys touch and the ends are facing upwards and downwards. Pull the feet downwards and inwards until the soles touch directly under the body and the arms go back to the starting position

♥ ♥ ♥ ♥ Increase the power on the pull down.

The Handbuoys increase the resistance

🔑 Soles touch

Your own notes:

_____

_____

_____

Sitting Roll Overs

♥♥♥ Keep an upright body, back straight, handbuoys held in each hand with the end facing forwards and backwards. Extend the arms downwards and outwards slightly to balance the body, keeping the handbuoys under the water. Curl the knees up to the chest, keeping legs and feet together, roll the knees over to the right, back to centre and then over to the left. Try to aim for the thigh of the upper leg to reach the surface. Keep the abdominal muscles engaged throughout and try not to move the arms. All movement is from the waist.

♥♥♥♥ sit up more upright.

The Handbuoys increase the buoyancy and maintain balance

🗝 **Roll, sit, roll**

Your own notes:

_____

_____

_____

357

Horizontal Roll Overs

♥ ♥ ♥

Keeping a straight back and abdominal muscles engaged and a straight back. Handbuoys held in each hand with the end facing forwards and backwards. Extend the arms outward and keep a very slight bent elbow to protect the shoulder joint. Keep legs together, heels up to buttocks and roll form left to right, slightly submerging the handbuoy on the side that the knees are rolling to. Aim to get the upper thigh to the surface and keep the feet submerged. Control all the way through the exercise,

The Handbuoys increase the buoyancy

🔑 **Roll left, roll right**

Your own notes:

_____

_____

_____

358

Cheer Leaders

♥ ♥ ♥ Cross one handbuoy over the other and hold in the centre of the square just under the surface and in front of the body. Keep a long straight body, bring knees up to chest and kick upwards and outwards while pushing the handbuoys down in between the legs. Aim to get the toes out of the water. Pull legs back down straight so the toes point to the floor and repeat

♥ ♥ ♥ ♥ Softly point the toes forward to increase leg length.

The Handbuoys increases the buoyancy

🔑 **Stay balanced**

Your own notes:

_____

_____

_____

Long Tuck Splash

♥♥♥ Hold the handbuoys in each hand, the ends facing forwards and backwards. Hands lower than shoulders and the handbuoys submerged throughout. Legs together bring the knees up to the chest, turn the handbuoys so the ends are facing side to side, then push the handbuoys forward in line with the ankle bones. Pull the handbuoys backwards towards the hips and at the same time flick the feet upwards to make a splash on the surface. Tuck the knees back to the chest and push the feet towards the floor, turn the handbuoys back so the ends face forwards and backwards. Repeat

♥♥♥♥ Softly point the toes forward to increase leg length.

The Handbuoys increases the resistance

🔑 **Knees up, splash**

Your own notes:

_____

_____

_____

Breaststroke Arm Cycle

♥♥♥ Sitting in the water, holding the handbuoys upright, ends pointing to the ceiling, back straight, and core muscles engaged.

As the legs make "cycling" movements the handbuoys are pushed forward in front of the body, pulled back towards the body and apart as the elbows tuck into the side of the ribs, the handbuoys come closer to the chest and closer to each other. Travel forwards.

♥♥♥♥ Increase the power and the speed and travel faster.

♥♥♥♥♥ Change direction of travel but always face forwards.

The Noodle increases resistance

🔑 **Drive with the heels**

Your own notes:

_____

_____

_____

Back Curl High Kicks

♥♥♥ Hold the handbuoys in each hand, the ends facing out to the sides, kick one leg forward and reach forward with the opposite arm to touch the toes, aim for the surface of the water, the other leg curls backwards with the knee pointing towards the pool floor. On the changeover of legs bring both arms down and the handbuoys to meet under the raised leg.

♥♥♥♥ Softly point the toes forward to increase leg length.

♥♥♥♥♥ Turn the handbuoys so the ends are facing forward as they meet under the kicking leg.

The Handbuoys increases the resistance

🔑 **Knees to pool floor**

Your own notes:

_____

_____

_____

Tricep Ski

♥ ♥ ♥ Long straight body, arms holding handbuoys in the centre with the ends facing forwards and backwards, Keep the shoulders down and the arms long, just wide of the body. Extend one leg forwards and the other leg backwards, on the changeover of the legs, pull the handbuoys upwards and inwards in line with the chest, but still submerged until they meet. As the legs changeover again, return the handbuoys to the start position.

♥ ♥ ♥ ♥ Softly point the toes forward to increase leg length.

♥ ♥ ♥ ♥ ♥ Increase the power and the speed.

The Handbuoys increases the resistance

🔑 **Long legs**

Your own notes:

_____

_____

_____

Pump Jogging

♥ ♥ Pump the legs up and down alternately, keeping the foot directly under the knee, use a flat foot. Hold the handbuoys with the end facing upwards and downwards, keep the elbows bent and pull and push the handbuoys in opposition to the legs. Right knee up left handbuoy forward. Travel in a forward facing direction.

♥ ♥ ♥ Increase the speed.

♥ ♥ ♥ ♥ Use direction changes to create turbulence.

The Handbuoys increases the resistance

🔑 **Power own soft knees**

Your own notes:

_____

_____

_____

Pull Downs

♥ ♥ ♥ Long straight body, arms holding handbuoys in the centre with the ends facing forwards and backwards, Keep the elbows slightly bent to avoid shoulder injury , shoulders down and the arms long and wide. The handbuoys must stay submerged.

Extend one leg forwards and the other leg backwards, on the changeover of the legs, pull the handbuoys in towards the body. As the legs changeover again, return the handbuoys to the start position with control so they do not "pop" out of the water.

♥ ♥ ♥ ♥ Increase the power and the speed.

The Handbuoys increases the buoyancy

🔑 **Long legs**

Your own notes:

_____

_____

_____

Resisted Cycles

❤❤❤ Sit in the water and use a cycling motion with the legs. Keep the body from leaning forward. Hold the handbuoys hip width apart behind the body with a light grip fingers facing towards the body and bent elbows. The end caps face out to the sides. Push the handbuoys down as far as comfortable, keeping the elbows bent and not allowing the handbuoys to touch the body.

❤❤❤❤ Increase the power and the speed of the legs.

❤❤❤❤❤ To Increase the drag hold the handbuoys wider apart.

The Handbuoys increases the buoyancy and cause drag

 Peddle

Your own notes:

_____

_____

_____

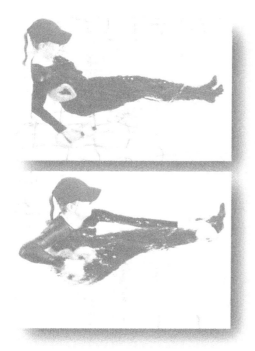

Crunch Touch

♥ ♥ ♥ Sit upright in the water, legs full extend out front. Abdominal muscles engaged throughout. Try to get the toes out of the water and keep them there. Lean backwards slightly. Hold the handbuoys with the ends facing forwards and backwards. Raise one handbuoy to just under the surface while the other handbuoy reaches forward towards the feet. Keep the back straight and avoid leaning. Pull both handbuoys back to the start position and repeat with the other handbuoy reaching forward.

♥ ♥ ♥ ♥ Increase the power.

The Handbuoys increases the buoyancy and resistance

🔑 **Straight legs**

Your own notes:

_____

_____

_____

Snow Angel Crunch

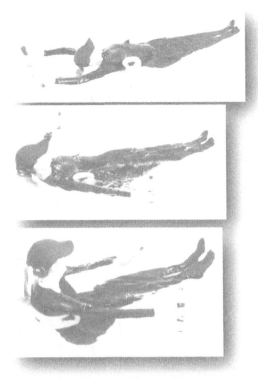

♥ ♥ ♥ Start supine, by being on your back stretched out fully in the water with the toes above the surface. Arms extended as far as comfortable above the head, with the handbuoys held with the end facing outwards. Engage core muscles and slowly push the buttocks to the pool floor while scooping the handbuoys down towards the hips. *The handbuoys must remain in the water throughout.* Aim to sit upright as much as possible by pushing the buttocks down further. Keeping a straight back, abs tight and toes out push the handbuoys towards the feet and keeping them at the side of the legs submerged. Hold, relax and return to start position, repeat.

♥ ♥ ♥ ♥ Increase the power of the scoop.

The Handbuoys increases the resistance

 Toes out

Your own notes:

_____

_____

_____

Long Kick Backs

♥♥♥ Leaning slightly forward in the deep, keeping the core engaged and the back straight. Bend the elbows holding the handbuoys so the end caps face up and down. Bring one knee up to the chest holding the handbuoys close to the body, kick the other leg straight out behind at and angle so the heels, hips and shoulders remain in a straight line. At the same time push the submerged handbuoys forwards, pull handbuoys back, bring knee up to chest and repeat with the other leg.

♥♥♥♥ Increase the speed.

The Handbuoys increases the resistance

🔑 **Back straight**

Your own notes:

_____

_____

_____

Sit Ups

♥ ♥ ♥

Supine with toes just above the surface, handbuoys held by the side of the body, end caps facing sideways. Abdominal muscles engaged. Push the bottom down to the pool floor, while curling th feet under the knees and pushing the handbuoys forward so they are in front of the body, Keep the back straight and the abdominal muscles engaged bring the feet and the hips back to the surface and recline fully. Repeat

♥ ♥ ♥ ♥ Increase the power.

The Handbuoys increases the resistance

🔑 **Push bottom down**

Your own notes:

_____

_____

_____

Tucked Twists

♥ ♥ ♥ Sitting in the water, knee raised and feet tucked under buttocks. Hold the handbuoys in an upright position with the endcaps facing top and bottom. Keep the handbuoys as close together as possible with bent arms, twist the knees to the left and pull the handbuoys through the water to the right. Make sure the knees are low enough to pull the handbuoys across the body. Twist the knees to the right and pull the handbuoys to the left, keeping the back straight.

♥ ♥ ♥ ♥ Increase the power and create turbulence.

The Handbuoys increases the resistance

🔑 **Pull**

Your own notes:

_____

_____

_____

Additional Lesson Plans
Deep Water Mitt Lesson Plan 1 hour session

A deep Water Workout using the aqua mitts to increase upper body resistance. The mitts have 3 levels of intensity. Throughout level 1 to 3 the wrist should be held firm to avoid strain or RSI (repetitive strain injury)

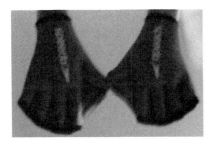

The flat hand (slicing) is level one, this offers the minimum resistance to the water (smallest surface area) this hand position can be vertical or horizontal.
SLICING

Level 2 is cupping the hand, the fingers are slightly curled forward, th hand position needs to be turned to maintain level 2 pushing against the direction of the water. The hand can be balled into a fist to make this level easier, but not as easy as slicing.

CUPPING

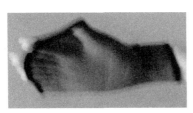

Level 3 Webbing, the fingers of the hand are extended open and the palm is flat, this level has the greatest resistance (also the greatest surface area)
WEBBING

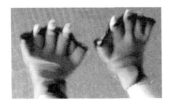

Like Webbing the pushing hand has a greater surface area, Beware of compromising the wrist by too much pushing

PUSHING

Warm Up

The hand position for the warm up starts with slicing, until the muscles are completely warm.

Legs - Jogging, Forward Kicks, Hamstring Curls, Ankle Taps, Heel Digs, Toe Taps, Straight Leg Kicks, Knee Lifts, Tyre Run, Lunges etc.,

Arms – Slicing through the water vertical and horizontal, mix and match with the leg movements.

Interval
Add speed, power, direction changes, cupping and webbing to this interval section. Propulsive static exercises to raise the heart rate, large power moves to tone the muscles. Maintain Centre of Gravity & Centre of Buoyancy to avoid injury!
Exercises –

C	Skis travel - cupped
A	Static Vertical propulsive tuck skis – webbed
C	Travel Long straight legs toes out – breaststroke arms webbed
A	Travel Sprinting – cupped and scooping the water
C	Static knee raisers and webbed hand clap under alternate knees
A	Static Vertical flutters – cupped / webbed
C	Static Horizontal Toe touches – slicing
A	Static Power cycle, reverse breaststroke arms – cupped
C	Travel Power cycle – webbed
A	Static Ski Legs – breaststroke arms – webbed
C	Travel cycle legs, anchored arms – webbed
A	Static Deep water Jax - slicing
C	Side scoops (one leg, one arm) – cupped reverse to use other leg and arm.
A	Travel in reverse Seated knees to chest, toes on surface fast flutter punching arms (fist)
C	Static Cross over high – low- high – webbed sculling
C	Travel Crossed ankles, knees raised. Paddle arms – cupped
A	Static High kicks – slicing
C	Travel High kicks (reverse) – pushing webbed
A	Travel High kicks forward - pulling cupped
C	Travel Mermaid legs – webbed sculling
A	Static Frog Legs – back of hand sweeps out elbows bent, and sweeps in to cross over chest – webbed.

Cooldown

Abdominal Work

Knee swings sitting vertically in the water, draw knees to chest, engage abdominal muscles and heels to bottom, swing legs over to one side and back to centre ® then change sides

Side cycles lay on one side, push one hand towards pool floor rest other on hip, cycle in a forwards direct, roll over and repeat.

Body swings stay vertical, bring knees to chest, engage abdominal muscles, scoop arms and pull body into supine position, stretch, curl knees to chest push body vertical and repeat.

Push Outs In a seated position bring knees up to chest, extend arms in front webbed position finger pointed up. Push legs out to fully stretched with soft knees, keeping feet flexed whilst pulling hands back to hips webbed with fingers pointing downwards.

Torso swings from vertical, bend knees slightly. Abs engaged push feet upwards, keep knees slightly bent and power back to start position and tilt body forward slightly as legs extend behind. Stay in a 45-degree zone.

Stretch
Keep body aligned throughout the normal deep stretches

Shallow Handbuoys – 1 hour session

Warm Up (hand buoys - on the surface minimising resistance)

Legs	Arms
Low knee jog	single push pulls front
Heel digs	double push pulls front
Toe taps	double push pulls
Ankle taps	hand buoys to ankle (under surface)
Rear ankle taps	hand buoys behind to ankle
Mini jax	hand buoys pull down & in to waist
Fwd flutter (t)	shoulder squeezes
Mini back kicks (t)	shoulder squeezes
Midi Jax (t)	hand buoys to thighs
Maxi jax	hand buoys to front

Aerobic (rebound moves with hand buoys under surface) Body alignment reminders.

Power jog	jog arms	static
Power jog	jog arms	travel forward
Power jog	double arms	travel backward
Power kicks forward reach outs	static	
Power kicks forward reach outs	travel forward	
Power back kicks with knee lift	double punch arms	static
Back Kicks	double punch arms	circle
Side rocks	single reach out	static
Side rocks	cross over reach out static	
Side rocks	double cross over	¼ turns (if space allows)
Skis	travel forward	
Skis	travel backward	
½ tuck skis	static	
full tuck skis	double ski arms	static or travel
Power frogs	X hand buoys	static
Power frogs	X hand buoys	fwd travel
Power frogs travel	X hand buoys	turn and fwd
Rocking horses	breaststroke arms	static
Power horses	double pull arms	static / ¼ turns
Maxi jax	power arms	static
Maxi tuck jax	power arms	static
Side jumps	opposition	static

Conditioning   (suspended)

Jax
Tuck jax
Thigh squeezers

Skis	static / travel
Power cycle	arms by side
Power cycle surface	arms extended to rear below the
Reverse power cycle	
Seated flutters	(low legs)
Ab work	
Shoot through	handbuoys under water
Sitting Vs	handbuoys tuck under knees
Side cycles	one handbuoy held vertically under water under shoulder
Curl crunch	hand buoys under water, sit, and curl crunch
Cooldown /stretch	No handbuoys

1 Hour Progressive Shallow Water Exercise Session

Warm Up (12 minutes)
Body alignment   Erector spinae, core muscles, trapezius

Basic jog   jogging arms   *Hamstring/pecs/lats*
Low forward kicks   alternate   pushing   arms   palms   up
Gastrocnemius, Hamstrings, pecs, lats
Side rocks mini left to right   small side pushes double arm
Ab & Adductors, oblique's, deltoids
Side rocks mini travel side pushes single arms
as above
Low back kicks   speedball arms
Hip Flexors, quads ,deltoids
Mini Flutters forward low travel   sculling arms
Tibialis anterior, gastrocnemius, biceps & triceps
Hamstring curls   double sculling arms
Quads, tibialis anterior, pecs. Lats, biceps & triceps

Increase intensity a little more

Wide leg jog   double jogging arm
Knee high forward leg kicks   breaststroke arms
Sidekicks alternate   double push arms opposite side
Sidekicks alternate (travel)   single opposite arms across the
body
Lunges static   clap in front of body under water
                                        keep elbows bent on the pull

Bounce flutters

Interval Training (30 minutes)   aerobic conditioning

Toe touches   Back   straight   toes   to
opposite hand   **(progression bounce it)**
Ski   large and powerful   ski
arms   **(progression increase speed keep it
BIG)**
Speed sprint   small and fast
                        **(progression increase speed and knee
height)**
Single Leg Knee raisers   lift knee high as poss push
                                        water behind
                        (Progression add speed keep it HIGH)
Knee tucks   both knees to chest
                (Progression shoulders under and bounces)
Single Leg Knee raisers other leg lift knee high as poss push
water behind 2 hands

(Progression add speed keep it HIGH)

Tuck bounce side to side   arms balanced outstretched under water

(Progression hands on hips)

Alternate side kicks (soft knees)   double push arms to opp side

(Progression kick higher and faster)

Jelly legs push each leg out to the side sculling arms   fast

(Progression add speed and enlarge)

Tuck Jacks   jack arms

(Progression shoulders stay under water)

Bounce Tuck Jacks   hug knees back of hand leads out

(Progression bounce higher)

Rocking Horse   8 then ¼ turn & repeat

(Progression kick back higher)

Fwd kick right leg, back kick left leg punch out with opp fist

(Progression add a bounce)

Suspended cycle   Travel   Breaststroke arms

(Progression enlarge movements & speed)

Suspended flutter kick from knee Breaststroke arms

(progression increase speed)

Abdominal Work (10 minutes) - noodle

Basic crunches 24 reps   noodle around upper back, lay flat on water toes out, push bottom to pool floor and raise shoulder to toes

Shoot through 24 reps   hold noodle out in front, lie flat, pull noodle to chest and curl knees to chest, sit upright keeping noodle still, push noodle down onto body, lay back and stretch out, push noodle down onto body, curl legs, sit upright, push noodle forward and stretch out.

Pendulums   24 reps   wrap noodle around upper back, curl knees to chest, keeping arms straight out to each side, swing both legs together Out to one side, keeping in line with arms, stretch, pull legs back to centre and repeat the other side.

Body balance Stand in centre of noodle with noodle on pool floor but not feet, stand tall and straight, bounce up and down, progress to small mini jumps. Hands by sides if possible. Jump forward and backwards keeping balance

Stretch (hold for 20secs each) keep moving in-between stretches

Gastroc (calf) Stand hip width apart,take a step back, straighten back foot heel on floor and transfer weight down back leg

Quad Stand tall, hold 1 heel to bottom (theirs) knee facing pool bottom, scull with spare arm

Hamstring Stand tall, back straight: soft supporting leg, raise one leg up & out in line with shoulder, hold foot/ ankle/ thigh and curl toes towards knee.

Buttock Hold knee to chest as high as comfortable, soft supporting leg.

Hip Flexors Stand hip width apart, take a step back, straighten back foot heel off floor and transfer weight down back leg

Pectorals Stand tall, reach behind body and hold hands aiming for below bottom, drop shoulders and squeeze shoulder blades together. Jiggle legs whilst stretching

Rbrac Stretch one arm forward, soft elbow fingers upwards and pull fingers gently back

Triceps Place one hand over shoulder on upper back, use other hand to take elbow behind head (only as far as comfortable)

Lats Lift one arm above head and lean over to the opposite side

Music suggestion 132 bpm

Music

There are a lot of legalities and controversy regarding playing music in a public place in the UK.

The legalities first.

In order to play music to the public i.e. to your classes, you are governed by PPL (Phonographic Performance Ltd) they issue the licences to allow this.

This is a government body and the licence if needed can be purchased directly from them.

They charge per number of classes that are done on a yearly basis, as a portion of your licence fee is distributed to the copyright owners of the tracks that you play.

It does not allow you to copy music and play it to your classes. As soon as you physically copy a track(s) you are in breach of copyright laws. The fine for this is very high.

This is something PPL take very seriously and carry out vigorous regular checks around the country in all public pools and health clubs.

You will need to check with each and every pool you work for if you are covered by their PPL licence.

Most pools now do not require you to have your own licence since the PPL law changed. But check, as you are responsible for the music you play and it will be you that gets the fine, not the pool.

If you were to hire a pool privately i.e. a school or use your own pool or a friend's pool, and offer classes to anyone other than family you will have to buy your own PPL licence and complete the paperwork required.

You really need to use music that has been mixed professionally. This music has no gaps between tracks, the bpm (beats per minute) are listed on the cover and the cd usually lasts 45 minutes or an hour.

There are many ways to obtain this music, there are speciality companies that sell the CDs, and these vary in price depending on if a portion of the price is for the license or they are licence free.

You can download tracks to your MP3 or iPod, but only from specified fitness music companies, you can purchase tracks individually and sync them to the order you want them to play or purchase a whole cd. You can choose the bpm that suits your classes and mix the genre.

With water exercise the music is purely motivational. We do not work to the beat of the music as working against resistance everyone is working at their own speed.

Unless the music is very slow and you use every other beat to choreograph the movements, then it can become un motivational and fails achieve any results.

Many of the fitter participants will get bored and uninspired.

If the music is too fast, the participants may try to work to the beat, and all movements will become short lever and not use the properties of water, this too will become ineffective.

The usual tempo for water exercise is from 128 – 135 bpm. This gives a good motivational speed.

The style of the music needs to be upbeat, without a heavy base. The genre needs to suit the type and age group of the class.

Also on the market is PPL free music, designed for use in fitness. This music is made specifically for the bpm of each track and is non original artist music. But it has been professionally mixed, has no gaps between the tracks, bpms are listed and they do not need a PPL licence.

The only reservation and it's not a huge one, is that PPL or license free music is not by the original artists. In a studio that might make a difference, but with the general background noise of the pool, the water pumps are circulating the water, waterfalls, other users and general noise of the water moving as the participant exercise very few people notice. These can be bought as CDs or downloads

This music can be all the same bpm throughout, or a graduated bpm for warm up, aerobic etc., some are designed for interval training with a bpm accordingly.

Most water exercise training companies sell these CDs and if you use the internet, look up 'fitness music' but make sure before you purchase that it is legal in the country you are going to be teaching in. Countries have different legal requirements.

Make your music motivating, change it regularly and whatever you decide, have fun with your classes and they will have fun with you.

Self-Evaluation

Feedback is great but as we have said before, self-assessment is important. Use the form below to help you identify any areas that you might change.

Did you plan this session?

_____

_____

What did you use to plan the session?

_____

_____

Did the exercises meet the participant's needs?

_____

_____

How effective and motivational were you?

_____

_____

Did you make any adaptions to suit particular participant's needs?

_____

_____

How many progressions did you offer for *each* exercise?

_____

_____

In what section of the session were they offered (warm up)(Interval)(aerobic)(conditioning)?

_____

_____

How could you improve?

_____

_____

How could you change your instructing style to meet particular participants' needs?

_____

_____

Do you understand the pool safety operating procedure for this pool?

_____

_____

Did you use any equipment?   Yes / No

What equipment did you use and why?

_____

_____

_____

What difference did the equipment make?

_____

_____

_____

Did you get any feedback from the participants?

_____

_____

_____

Final Summary

Now we know what to do and how to do it, but the bigger question is why?

Why are your participants coming to your classes? What do your participants expect from you? The answer to that is a lot. They expect you to be punctual, friendly, approachable, professional, motivational, discreet, legal, well planned, fun, helping them achieve their goals and a lot more.

It helps if you know why they are there, as we have said before. Some come along for the social aspect, some to lose weight, some to get generally fitter, some because they have health issues, some because it's fun, some because they like you and your teaching style and some because if they don't do some exercise they stiffen up and it causes mobility problems.

It's your job to find out why they come, help them achieve their goals, motivate them to come again and try to make everyone part of the event so they don't want to miss out. Appointments can be booked around their fitness routine. Teach them fitness comes first.

It's a lot to ask of one person, but remember if you are not qualified to answer their questions, refer them to somebody who can. If they are having joint problems, refer them to their GP, Physio Therapist or the Wellness department if the centre has one.

To be the best you can be, you have to continually evaluate yourself, ask for feedback from the class, but at the end of the day you know how you performed. You know what could have been done better.

14 Point Performance Evaluation List: -
Were you / did you?

1. On Time and set up poolside

2. Enthusiastic and motivating

3. Good size and good speed demonstrations

4. Loud and clear verbal communication

5. Moving your teaching position around the pool

6. Corrections and motivation given

7. Lesson plans devised

8. All muscle groups catered for

9. Progressions given throughout

10. Adaptions given where necessary

11. Were your participants working at their own level?

12. Did they enjoy your music?

13. Were they enjoying the session?

14. What could you have done better?

Aqua Personal Training

We know how supportive the water is and all the benefits of water exercise, so what better way if you a have or want to get a Personal Trainers qualification and take this over to the water.

It's not just the long term joint problem sufferers who will benefit for this highly specialised 1-2-1 session. Anyone whose fitness matters to them will get excellent results.

Winter training for

- Runners
- Rugby players
- Footballers
- Cyclists
- Athletes

Endurance training

- Professional sports personnel
- Martial arts competitors
- Athletes

Aid injury recovery for

- Dancers
- Sports personnel
- Gymnasts
- Kick boxers
- Runners
- Cyclists

Personalised sessions for people who

- can't get to a class because of irregular shift work,
- people who don't want to exercise in a group
- people who need a personal trainer to motivate them

The lists are endless, and I am sure you can think of people you already know who would benefit from the experience of a 1-2-1 in the water when it's done properly.

A new avenue for the club you already work in, another string to your bow and extra revenue.

Do you have your own pool?

Other avenues:

There are many ways to enhance your aqua qualification. Take a specialist course in pre and post-natal and combine the two for pre and post-natal classes.

A GP referral qualification could allow you to add an aqua wellness class.

A dementia or mental health qualification could enable you to start a specialised session.

A ballet qualification could get you into cross training dancers, although you would need to modify the exercises.

Yoga or Pilate's qualification – Aqua yoga or aqua Pilates, again some modification will be needed as the water us too cool for normal yoga or Pilates classes and some exercises are just not possible in the water like a full sun salutation or downward dog.

Whatever you think of, it can normally be done with the right qualifications and quick check with your insurance company and of course the pool you want to run these sessions in.

Blank Lesson Plans

Warm Up 8 – 10 minutes

Exercise	Travel	Arm movement	Major Muscles	Progression	🔑
Warm Up					

Notes:

_____

_____

_____

_____

_____

Aerobic 30 minutes

Exercise	Travel	Arm movement	Major Muscles	Progression	🔍
Aerobic					

Notes:

_____

_____

_____

Conditioning 10 minutes

Exercise	Travel	Arm movement	Major Muscles	Progression	🔑
Conditioning					

Notes:

_____

_____

_____

_____

_____

Interval 40 minutes

Exercise	Travel	Arm movement	Major Muscles	Progression	🔑
Interval					

Notes:

_____

_____

_____

Abdominal section 10 minutes

Exercise	Travel	Arm movement	Major Muscles	Progression 🔑
Stretching				

Notes:

_____

_____

_____

_____

_____

Station	1	2	3	4	5	6
Circuit Lesson Plan						
Warm up						
Aerobic						
MSE						
Ab Work						
Stretch						
Fun						

Notes:

_____

_____

_____

_____

_____

Key   *s = shallow exercises*
sus = suspended
exercises
d = deep
sn = shallow noodles
sh = shallow
handbuoys
dn = deep noodles
dh = deep handbuoys

Appendix

396

397

Lightning Source UK Ltd.
Milton Keynes UK
UKOW07f1502220517
301749UK00005B/30/P

9 781909 465589